also from

aplomb publishing
San Francisco

Who Nuked the Duke

What Ever Happened to Mommie Dearest?

Alfred Hitchcock - The Icon Years

Reel Horror - True Horrors Behind Hollywood's Scary Movies

Curse of the Silver Screen - Tragedy & Disaster Behind the Movies

Master of Disaster - Irwin Allen: The Disaster Years

Disaster on Film - Behind the Scenes of Hollywood's Classic Disaster Films

www.aplombpublishing.com

Murder on the *Boob Tube*

By John William Law

aplomb publishing
San Francisco

Murder on the Boob Tube

Published by Aplomb Publishing, San Francisco, California.
Copyright 2015.

978-0-9825195-1-6

2nd edition

Manufactured in the United States of America.

No part of this publication may be reprinted without written permission from the publisher. For more information, write Aplomb Publishing, editor@aplombpublishing.com.

Dedicated to TV fans everywhere.

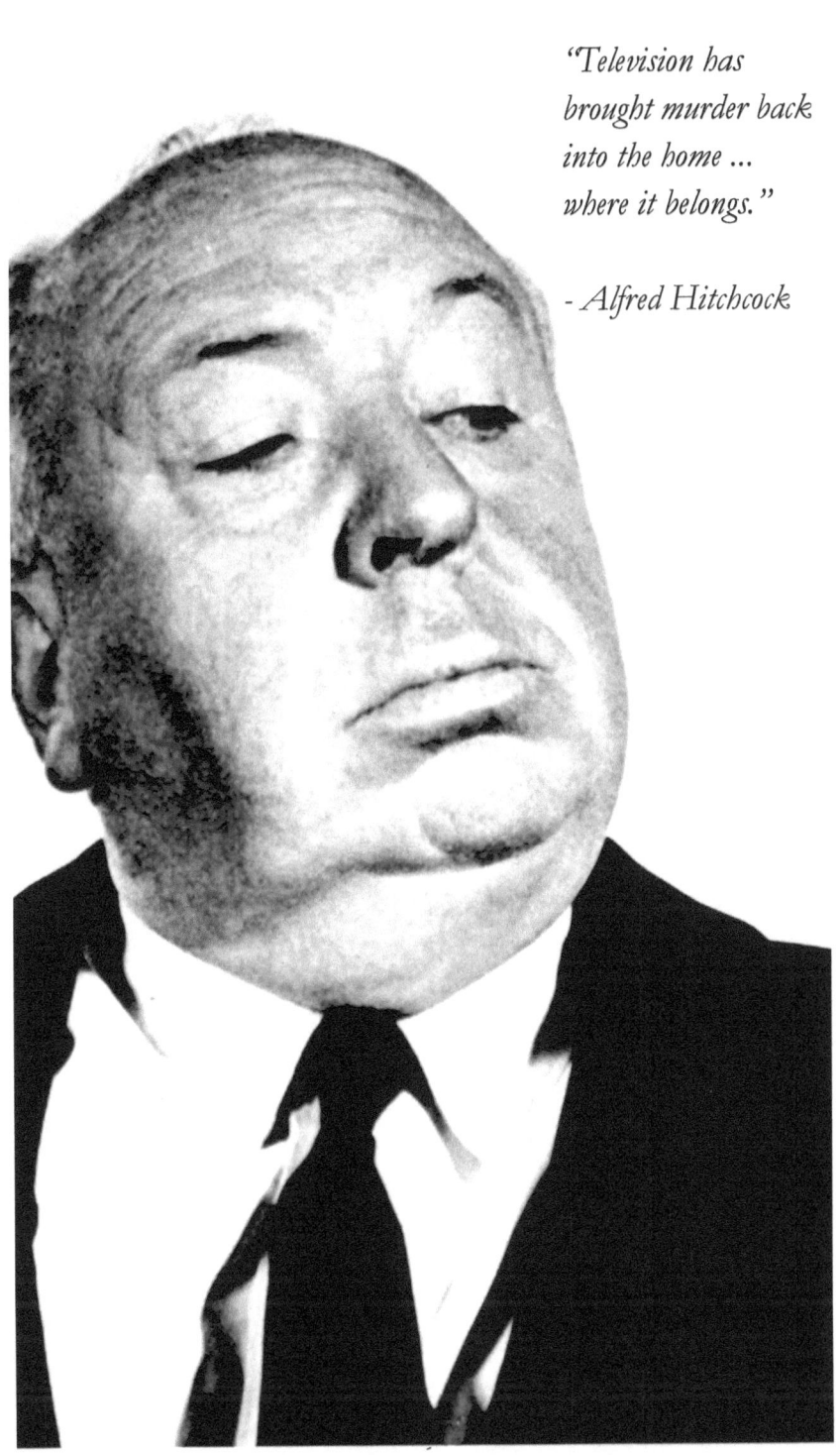

"Television has brought murder back into the home ... where it belongs."

- *Alfred Hitchcock*

Table of Contents

-	Opening Remarks	Page 13
-	About the Shows	Page 19
1	Introduction	Page 21
2	Alfred Hitchcock Presents	Page 27
3	Barnaby Jones	Page 37
4	Burke's Law	Page 47
5	Cannon	Page 55
6	Charlies Angels	Page 63
7	Columbo	Page 73
8	Dragnet	Page 83
9	Ellery Queen	Page 95
10	Hart to Hart	Page 103
11	Hawaii Five-O	Page 113
12	Ironside	Page 121
13	Mannix	Page 131
14	McCloud	Page 139
15	McMillan & Wife	Page 147
16	Perry Mason	Page 155
17	Quincy, ME	Page 163
18	The Streets of San Francisco	Page 173
19	Also Rans	Page 183
20	The New Breed	Page 199
-	Closing Remarks	Page 209

Appendix

sources	Page 215
index	Page 223

MURDER on the Boob Tube

MURDER on the Boob Tube

Preface

MURDER on the Boob Tube

Opening Remarks

A mystery about to unfold

As television shows become a part of our pop culture psyche the actors who bring the roles to life become iconic figures for fans and television audiences. It's virtually impossible to imagine anyone other than Peter Falk inhabiting the role of Lt. Columbo, but in reality several other actors played the part before him, one on stage and another in a television teleplay. And when producers set their sights on giving the detective his own series, it wasn't Falk they had in mind ... believe it or not it was Bing Crosby.

MURDER on the Boob Tube

When *Hart to Hart* was being developed it was the image of Cary Grant that the writers and producers had pictured in the role, but Grant was well past his prime at that point and it was unlikely he'd take part in a weekly series. Robert Wagner was approached about the role and accepted the part.

Many actresses tested for would-be angels in the *Charlie's Angels* phenomenon of the 70s. But it was Kate Jackson, Jaclyn Smith and Farrah Fawcett who became television superstars. Kim Basinger didn't get one of the parts, but did end up guest starring in one of the first season's most memorable episodes. In later seasons as actresses exited their starring roles and producers sought to replace Fawcett, Jackson and others, many actresses were again considered. Can you imagine Kathie Lee Gifford or Michelle Pfeiffer with gun in hand taking down the bad guys? It might have happened had producers given them a shot after their auditions for the series.

Another show whose star really set the style of the series was Jack Lord when he led his team of police officers for a decade uncovering corruption and crime in paradise in *Hawaii Five-O*. But Lord was not what producers wanted when they hoped to lure Gregory Peck to weekly television. But Peck wasn't interested and a search went on for his replacement. Lord was a last-minute choice, and the rest is history.

Many other casting coups and interesting choices surrounding shows like *Murder She Wrote, Mannix* and others have also been reported over the years.

As a pop-culture junkie I've long been fascinated with behind-the-scenes tales of Hollywood. My attention was mostly relegated to film history and the making of motion pictures. But as an avid fan of television dramas and mysteries, I grew up watching cop shows, detective shows and the general whodunits that so regularly came across the TV networks.

It eventually seemed fitting that I would turn my attention to television. I decided looking back at many of the shows I grew up on and the stars who gave them life would be a fascinating project. With many of these shows still turning up on cable networks as well as DVD they seem to still be finding audiences and fans. And while some of them don't hold up with the technical capabilities and production budgets of today's TV productions, the shows provided the formative years of TV and without them many of the shows we enjoy today might not be possible. Even with the dated images, often silly plot lines and sometimes less-than-epic action sequences, the shows hold a certain level of charm and innocence.

While today the image of corpses and death are commonplace in show's like *CSI* today, only a few short decades ago Jack Klugman's *Quincy, M.E.* wasn't even able to show a dead corpse he was examining in the morgue. There's something to be said for a kinder, gentler era.

I hope you enjoy the look back at TV history.

- John William Law, author

MURDER on the Boob Tube

About the Shows

A tribute to murder on the small screen

Note that following the introduction a series of some of the most memorable shows are chronicled with a look behind each series. Shows were selected for their impact on television and for their focus on murder as a prime component of the story lines of most of the episodes.

In addition each is introduced with a brief look at their broadcast histories and cast line-ups. We aimed to as accurately as possible detail the airing history of each show. The information comes from various sources. In addition to the sources listed in the back of this book, airing dates in some cases come from network reports, production and DVD list data, *TV Guide* annual network listings and *TVs Greatest Hits: The 150 Most Popular Shows of All Time*. Shows are listed in alphabetical order and not chronologically or by importance or other ranking.

And to pay tribute to the countless other shows with murder as a focus we detail both the earlier and also-ran shows that ran alongside those we've detailed and we follow that with a chapter on the "New Breed" of shows that came later, continuing the tradition of murder on the small screen.

While we aimed to capture as many of the shows as possible, we expect we have missed a few, but even for those not chronicled here, this book is a tribute to them all.

MURDER on the Boob Tube

MURDER on the Boob Tube

MURDER on the Boob Tube

Introduction

A new medium and to coin a phrase

In 1961 President John F. Kennedy appointed attorney Newton N. Minow as one of seven commissioners to the Federal Communications Commission. And that same year Minow gave what would be his most memorable speech calling television programming of the day a "vast wasteland." The speech has been called one of the hundred best speeches of the 20th Century and would help define, if not scar, television for the remainder of the century.

Newton's opinion of television was that it held great potential, suggesting that "arguably TV was created to serve public interest, but now it can be seen more in character of the "boob tube," a mindless occupation and time filler."

With that remark, the TV set was rechristened "the boob tube" and the phrase has stuck. While the social impact of television has been a topic of great discussion for decades so has the criticism of much of the programming that came from its airwaves.

"When television is good, nothing — not the theater, not the magazines or newspapers — nothing is better," Minow said. "But when television is bad, nothing is worse. I invite you to sit down in front of your television set when your station goes on the air and stay there, for a day, without a book, without a magazine, without a newspaper, without a profit and loss sheet or a rating book to distract you. Keep your eyes glued to that set until the station signs off. I can assure you that what you will observe is a vast wasteland."

Minow would become a part of the pop culture phenomenon just a few years later in 1964 when producer Sherwood Schwartz remembered Minow's speech and used him as an inspiration of sorts when he delivered the pilot of his situation comedy *Gilligan's Island* to CBS. He named the tiny ship that strands seven castaways on an island as the S.S. Minnow, not specifically after the fish that many suspected, but rather in honor of Newton Minow and his view of television.

Newton Minow helped coin the phrase, "The Boob Tube" in the early 1960s.

The Early Days

But television had a long road to travel before meeting the cross hairs of Minow's memorable speech. Back as far as 1923 it was being discussed in the board rooms of entertainment programming organizations. David Sarnoff, founder of NBC was head of RCA in 1923 when he drafted a memorandum for the board of directors of RCA predicting "Television will make it possible for those at home to see as well as hear what is going on at the broadcast station."

While television was practically unheard of at time by the average citizen, radio was about to catch on in a big way. It was December 12, 1901 that Guglielmo Marconi launched a kite into the sky that had a series of wires attached to it turning it into a would-be antenna. With coastal winds in his favor the kite remained air born and at a prearranged time that afternoon he used a pair of earphones to listen for a sound. When he heard three faint dots signaling the "S" in Morse code he discovered his "wireless" transmission had worked and his invention would forever change the world. Soon, the ability to transmit not only wireless code, but spoken words and music around the world.

But what many also suspected was if you could transmit sound wirelessly then it was certainly possible to transmit images. Scientists just had to figure out how.

It would begin to happen as early as 1906 when the concept of a cathode-ray tube was being developed. The forerunner to the television picture tube the idea would take years to realize and around 1923 Vladimir Zworykin would accomplish the task with his "Iconoscope."

The name "television" was taking hold as the delivery model for the images and the technology would soon be in full-fledged development. Sarnoff was referring to his concept of "television" as "the art of distant seeing" and the name came from a marriage of Greek and Latin terms with "tele" coming from the Greek term for "far-off" and "visio" from the Latin term for "to see."

As experiments of transmitting or telecasting signals began to take place around 1927 and 28 and further development of the device for receiving these signals would carry on into the 1930s.

By the 1939 World's Fair visitors were seeing their first glimpse of the future and a device called the "television" and election returns on November 15, 1940 were telecast for the first time. By the spring of 1941 the first television license was granted by the Federal Communications Commission to NBC.

In 1947 only about 14,000 homes held television sets, but broadcasters knew things were about to change and programming began to take on greater scale as word of mouth began to carry the message of TV across the country and around the world. They were right and in 1948 there were some 175,000 TV sets in homes and just a few years later, by 1953 there were 20 million television receivers in America. And by then, programming had evolved from simple news and information delivery to entertainment programming. And one of the most watched types of programming was the mystery-suspense genre and the good old-fashioned murder had found a home on what would soon be called "the boob tube."

MURDER on the Boob Tube

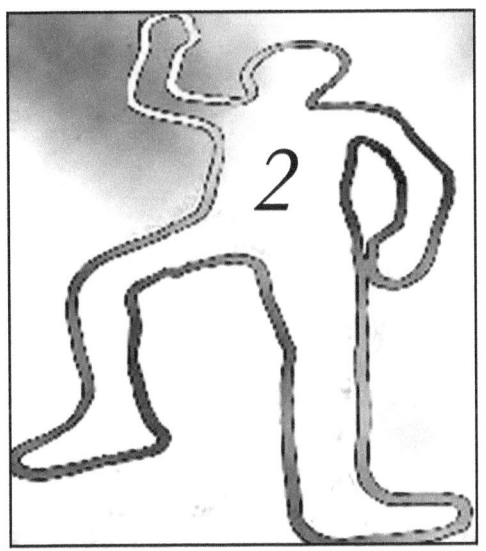

MURDER on the Boob Tube

MURDER on the Boob Tube

Alfred Hitchcock Presents
Suspense Anthology

First telecast: October 2, 1955
Final telecast: September 6, 1965

Broadcast History:
October 1955-September 1960, CBS, Sunday 9:30-10:00 pm
September 1960-September 1962, NBC Tuesday 8:30-9:00 pm
September 1962-December 1962, CBS Thursday 10:00-11:00 pm
January 1963-September 1963, CBS Friday 9:30-10:30 pm
September 1963-September 1964, CBS Friday10:00-11:00 pm
October 1964-September 1965, NBC Monday 10:00-11:00pm

Host:
Alfred Hitchcock

Additional Title:
The Alfred Hitchcock Hour

MURDER on the Boob Tube

MURDER on the Boob Tube

Alfred Hitchcock Presents

Good evening, ladies & gentlemen

Alfred Hitchcock's name had been a headline on the marquee for decades but by the mid 1950s he would be welcomed into America's living rooms with a weekly TV series *Alfred Hitchcock Presents*. The show debuted in the fall season of 1955 and would grow on TV viewers into a top rated series by the end of the decade. As the 60s came into view his show was going as strong as ever. While he didn't direct most of the episodes his story selections and his introductions of them made him one of the most recognizable faces in Hollywood

MURDER on the Boob Tube

– often more so than many of his stars.

His deadpan and often droll delivery of his introductory messages often went something like this:

> "Good evening, ladies and gentlemen, and welcome to darkest Hollywood. Night brings stillness to the jungle. It is so quiet, you can hear a name drop. The savage beasts have already begun gathering at the water holes to quench their thirst. Now one should be especially alert. The vicious table-hopper is on the prowl, and the spotted back-biter may lurk behind a potted palm."

And if that wasn't enough he used the popularity of the series to develop a successful series of paperback books from Dell Publishing. Collections of short stories, written by others, that carried his brand of suspense suspended by twists and turns, were pocketbook favorites that kept him front and center in bookstores everywhere. Along with his se-

Alfred Hitchcock delivered his series to the public for nearly a decade.

ries, they helped make him a very wealthy man even when his big screen features didn't always make it big at the box office.

With roughly 30-years of film experience his name would draw attention to the relatively new medium of television drama and once it did, his face became better known than many of his actors.

Although he only directed 17 half-hour or hour-long episodes of his show, the series would air a reported 350 episodes, and like his books, he would be putting his face on every episode, almost stamping the work of others as his own. It was his style and his show. And one of the trademarks of the series was the iconic Hitchcock silhouette, which reportedly came from a sketch used for a Christmas card designed by Hitchcock himself.

A Ratings Hit

The show would do quite well in the ratings during its first few seasons, moving between fourth and sixth place, behind staples like *The Ed Sullivan Show* and *Lucy*. In its second season it would earn an Emmy Award for writing. The series would also prove financially rewarding. Hitchcock's contact would earn him $129,000 per show, as well as all rights of sale and rebroadcast after each show first aired. For filming he set up a television company, Shamley Productions, named after a summer home he and his wife purchased in Shamley Green, a small village south of London, back in 1928. Hitch's contract with Bristol-Meyers stipulated that he would only direct an "unspecified number of episodes" each season.

His shows also featured a host of memorable guest stars. Including many of his film actors, like Vera Miles, Norman Lloyd, and Barbara Belle Geddes, to other notable stars including Joseph Cotton, Claud Rains, Walter Matthau, Virginia Gregg, Brian Keith, Darren McGavin, Hume Cronyn, Mary Wickes, Peter Lorre and William Shatner.

MURDER on the Boob Tube

It aired on CBS from 1955 until 1960 when it was picked up by NBC in 1960. After two seasons on NBC, CBS brought the show back to its network, but this time as an hour-long show and renaming it *The Alfred Hitchcock Hour*. Its final season, in 1964, would be on NBC, also in an hour-ling format.

Hitchcock's TV series crew and production company helped bring life to his 1960 classic film 'Psycho.'

Hitch would also direct two other noteworthy television shows during this period. One was an episode of a drama called *Suspicion* in 1957 and the other was an episode of *Ford Star Time* in 1960. His television work allowed him to keep a schedule, something his film actors would grow accustomed to on his later films. He ended his day at 4 p.m. and enjoyed the regularity of a schedule. His half-hour dramas were filmed in three days and the hour-long shows in five. And even though he didn't direct the bulk of the shows he left his mark was left on each. He selected each show that would be filmed and oversaw much of the key production decisions. He would even employ many members of his TV crew on future film work and a number of the actors in his shows would find their way into his films.

A Series in Motion

As the series progressed it jumped networks, moving from CBS to NBC and the back to CBS. In addition, the format was extended from a half-hour short story to an hour-long extended edition. Viewers would certainly struggle to keep up with not only the time of the airing each season, but the network. As viewership dropped the network became less inclined to bankroll a new season of production.

The series ended the 1964-65 season with a final airing on September 6, 1965. The expense of the show and its costly star weighed the series down and newer shows like *The Outer Limits* and *The Twilight Zone* offered similar fare.

But it was his personality, his name and his face on the movie screen, the TV screen and in bookstores, presenting the Hitchcock brand of macabre suspense. And this would help make him an icon. He would put the director's role on the map and turned himself into a television and movie star. His image would be recognizable across the globe and he would be one of the most popular and successful personalities in Hollywood. The series still finds its way onto television today and has also been remade into new shows and released on DVD.

And his TV series production company would also take part in his most successful feature film when he used it for the making of *Psycho* which would break box office records around the world after its release in 1960.

MURDER on the Boob Tube

MURDER on the Boob Tube

MURDER on the Boob Tube

Barnaby Jones
Detective Drama

First telecast: January 28, 1973
Final telecast: September 4, 1980

Broadcast History:
January-June 1973, CBS, Sunday 9:30-10:30 pm
July-September 1974, CBS Saturday 10:00-11:00 pm
September 1974-August 1975, CBS Tuesday 10:00-11:00 pm
September-November 1975, CBS Friday 10:00-11:00 pm
December 1975-November 1979, CBS Thursday 10:00-11:00 pm
December 1979-September 1980, CBS Thursday 9:00-10:00 pm

Cast:
Barnaby Jones: Buddy Ebsen
Betty Jones: Lee Merriweather
Jedediah Romano "JR" Jones (1976-1980): Mark Shera
Lt. Biddle (1974-1980): John Carter

Executive Producer:
Quinn Martin

MURDER on the Boob Tube

Barnaby Jones

Bartender, make that a glass of milk

Buddy Ebsen's career in Hollywood started as far back as the early 1930s. By the mid-part of the decade he was acting in a host of feature films like *Broadway Melody of 1936*, *Born to Dance* and *My Lucky Star*. When he lost the role of the Tin Man in *The Wizard of Oz* because the heavy paint caused him to become terribly ill, he moved onto more roles in forgettable films but would later find himself regular work on the new medium of television.

With guest starring roles in all sorts of shows like *Stars over Hollywood, Broadway Television Theater, Schlitz Playhouse of Stars,*

Disneyland and *Maverick* he found steady work. And after a supporting role in the hit film *Breakfast at Tiffany's* in 1961 he would move into what would become one of his most famous roles. From 1962 until 1971 he was the star of *The Beverly Hillbillies*, a situation comedy that made him a household name, a star and a financially successful actor.

After *The Beverly Hillbillies* ended its run in 1971 Ebsen continued working regularly as guest star in many 1970s TV shows, many of which were dramas like *Cannon, Night Gallery* and *Hawaii Five-O*, as well as TV movies like *The Horror at 37,000 Feet* and *Smash-Up on Interstate Five*.

But regular series work would come calling again when he accepted the starring role in a new dramatic series called *Barnaby Jones* in 1973. And at the time it was reported that Ebsen was one of the oldest TV stars on series television.

Buddy Ebsen and Lee Merriweather starred in 'Barnaby Jones.'

MURDER on the Boob Tube

Barnaby Jones was a television detective show with Ebsen in the title role, alongside former Miss America Lee Meriwether as his daughter-in-law. Both were private investigators solving murders and a host of criminal activities in the Los Angeles area where the series was set.

The detective show ran on CBS from January 28, 1973 until April 3, 1980. It reportedly started as a midseason replacement and got a following from a lead-in audience already tuned in for the long-running detective series *Mannix*, which aired before it. But *Barnaby Jones* has another detective to thank for his rise to fame. The *Barnaby Jones* character was first introduced to CBS viewers in 1973 in an episode of the William Conrad detective series *Cannon*.

No Retirement for the Sleuth

The premise of the show centered on Jones who after many years as a private eye decides to retire, leaving his business to his son Hal. After Hal is murdered while working on a case, Barnaby comes out of

Buddy Ebsen was the popular sleuth on CBS with Lee Merriweather as his daughter-in-law assisting him.

retirement to find his son's killer. With help from his widowed daughter-in-law, Betty Jones, the duo solve the case and find that they work so well together they decide to continue in business together and keep the detective agency open.

In 1976 actor Mark Shera joined the cast as the character of J.R., son of Barnaby's cousin. Shera brought more youth and action into the series when he came to solve the murder of his father, but remained at Barnaby's side while the character of Betty attended law school.

'Barnaby Jones' would grace the cover of TV Guide numerous times during its run on CBS.

Jones was unlike most hard-drinking detectives, opting for milk instead of liquor and he was known for using his intellect to break his cases open instead of his brawn. While he wasn't known for his virility he seldom ended up in fights though occasional gunfire would have him dodging for cover. He was also often known for lulling the guilty into a false sense of security which gave him the opportunity to let them incriminate themselves.

The show was also known for its plethora of guest stars. A who's who of television actors appeared during the show's run, including recognizable names and faces like Stefanie Powers, Wayne Rogers, William Shatner, Leslie Nielsen, Richard Anderson, Claude Akins, Vera Miles, Meredith Baxter-Birney, Bill Bixby, Larry Hagman, Jack Cassidy, Geraldine Brooks, Dabney Coleman, Jackie Coogan, Cathy Lee Crosby, Anne Francis, Lynda Day George, Richard Hatch, Margot Kidder, Ida Lupino, Roddy McDowell, George Maharis, Nick Nolte, and Jessica Walter.

As the series dragged on Ebsen began to find the pace of the series difficult to keep up with. So, with his agreement, Meriwether and Shera's characters became much more prominent, lessening Ebsen's workload.

Ebsen once said in and interview "For *Barnaby Jones*, I owned the set. When I walked on the set I was the most important man… I was the star of the show. And I got to contribute to some of the stories."

It was ultimately low ratings that lead to the show's cancellation in 1980, but Ebsen had actually had enough of playing the title role and the end was a welcome one. The series also moved around the network time schedule numerous times during its run which sometimes made it difficult for fans to keep up with its timeslot.

In the mid 1990s, with the successful returns of other classic detectives like *Columbo* and *Perry Mason*, there was some interest in doing the same for *Barnaby Jones*. Both Lee Meriwether and Mark Shera reportedly expressed interest in a *Barnaby Jones* reunion TV movie. But Buddy Ebsen was unable to be convinced to return to the role. But in 1993, he would actually reprise the role he made famous when Ebsen played the character of Barnaby Jones in the feature-film remake of his other famous TV series, *The Beverly Hillbillies*. It would mark his final big screen appearance, though he continued to make occasional TV appearances through the remainder of the decade including his final series *Matt Houston* which aired in 1994. Ebsen died in 2003 at the age of 95, but *Barnaby Jones* lives on in television history through syndication and DVD releases.

It was an ensemble cast for 'Barnaby Jones' but Ebsen was always its star.

MURDER on the Boob Tube

MURDER on the Boob Tube

MURDER on the Boob Tube

Burke's Law
Law Drama

First telecast: September 20,1963
Final telecast: January 12, 1966

Broadcast History:
September 1963-May 1964, ABC Friday 8:30-9:30 pm
September 1964-April 1965, ABC Wednesday 9:30-10:30 pm
September 1965-January 1966, ABC Wedneday 10:00-11:00 pm

Cast:
Amos Burke: Gene Barry
Detective Tim Tilson: Gary Conway
Detective Les Hart: Regis Toomey,
Sergeant Ames: Eileen O'Neill
Henry the chauffeur: Leon Lontoc
George McCloud: Michael Fox

Producer:

Aaron Spelling

MURDER on the Boob Tube

MURDER on the Boob Tube

Burke's Law

Who killed so-and-so?

Gene Barry was a familiar face on television by the early 1960s. Having appeared as a guest star in many televisions shows he was also a regular on popular shows like *Our Miss Brooks, Ford Television Theatre, Jane Wyman Presents The Fireside Theatre* and *Bat Masterson*. But in 1963 he stepped into the role of Amos Burke in *Burke's Law* and became a staple of the ABC line-up from 1963 to 1966.

The main character, Amos Burke actually first appeared in 1961 in an episode of *The Dick Powell Show* and was played by Powell himself. *Burke's Law* was spin-off of sorts from the original concept. The series was produced by Powell's Four Star Television and featured Barry as a millionaire who was chauffeured around to solve crimes in a Rolls-Royce. In fact, Dick Powell may very well have continued as the star of the series had he not died of cancer in early 1963. The character was known for dispensing wisdom to his underlings as he went about solving his crimes. Statements like "Never ask a question unless you already know the answer," were commonplace during the show's run.

Each episode started with "Who Killed..." followed by a name or description of the victim. The killing was almost always shown in the first few minutes of the show and Burke's role was to bring about justice by the closing credits.

In the original series, beside Barry, supporting roles features Detective Tim Tilson played by Gary Conway, Detective Les Hart played by Regis Toomey, Sergeant Ames played by Eileen O'Neill, and Leon Lontoc who played Henry, Burke's Asian chauffeur. Tilson was chief rival for Burke, but his ability to find clues didn't result in solving the

Gene Barry, center, with costars in 'Burke's Law.'

murders, as it would be up to Burke and his keen intuition and detective skills that shed light on the truth behind each crime.

Re-Tooling the Series

After the 64-65 season the show was re-tooled and for the final season of 1965–1966 the show was renamed *Amos Burke, Secret Agent* with Burke going to work for a secret government agency. Trying to capitalize on the successful James Bond film series, Burke's became a secret agent but he still drove around in his Rolls Royce, but now it had been bullet-proofed. He was out of his job with the San Francisco Police Department and employed as international espionage agent who received his orders from a mysterious man aboard a plane. However, the changes didn't help the series, which didn't run a full season. Only seventeen episodes were aired before the show was cancelled.

In one of the standout episodes in the first season in 1963 and then again in 1965 Anne Francis appeared as female detective Honey West, which became a spin-off detective series named after the title character in 1965. *Honey West* co-starred John Ericson and last only one season in 1965.

In 1994 with a revival on television of aged detectives like those in *Matlock*, *Diagnosis Murder*, and *Murder She Wrote*, as well as familiar appearances of *Columbo* and *Perry Mason*, CBS dusted off Amos Burke and revived the series for one season 1994-1995. Barry returned as his rich police detective Burke, alongside his son Peter, played by Peter Barton.

This time series only lasted one season but featured notable guest appearances by many familiar faces from 1960s television, including Patrick Macnee from *The Avengers*, Peter Lupus of *Mission: Impossible* and Anne Francis who came back as a version of her character from *Honey West*.

MURDER on the Boob Tube

The first season of *Burke's Law* featured 32 episodes and has since been released on DVD along with the spin-off *Honey West*, also on DVD, allowing new viewers to see the series for the first time and old viewers to rediscover the Gene Barry classic.

MURDER on the Boob Tube

MURDER on the Boob Tube

MURDER on the Boob Tube

Cannon
Detective Drama

First telecast: September 14, 1971
Final telecast: September 19, 1976

Broadcast History:
September 1971-September 1972, CBS, Tuesday 9:30-10:30 pm
September 1972-September 1973 CBS Wednesday 10:00-11:00 pm
September 1973-July 1976, CBS Wednesday 9:00-10:00 pm
July 1976-September 1976, CBS Sunday 10:00-11:00 pm

Cast:
Frank Cannon: William Conrad

Executive Producer:
Quinn Martin

MURDER on the Boob Tube

Cannon

Watch out for the unassuming fat guy

Cannon was cut from the cloth of many other detective dramas of the 60s and 70s. While he was much less an action figure than Joe Mannix, he was more able-bodied than a Robert T. Ironside. His frank talk and keen observation skills made him a successful adversary for those he was up against.

The detective series ran on CBS from 1971 to 1976 and starred William Conrad as the overweight detective Frank Cannon. Conrad showed up in Hollywood in the 1940s and found himself cast as a policeman, a villain or any number of small supporting roles in a host of forgettable B-movies through the 1950s. While *Sorry Wrong Number* was probably one of his most memorable films, other features like *The Conqueror* or countless westerns and film noir quickies kept him working until work in television provided him with more steady work and meatier roles.

It was his voice that first found him success. As narrator of *This Man Dawson* and *Rocky and His Friends*, both in 1959-1960 as well as later in *The Bullwinkle Show* and *Geronimo*, he found his deep and bold voice one that translated well on TV even if his portly appearance did not. In fact had Conrad looked more like leading-man material he might have ended up as the star of an even bigger show. On radio, Conrad was the voice of the marshall in *Gunsmoke*, but his appearance wasn't suitable to the onscreen persona when the series was brought to television and James Arness would be cast in the career-making role.

William Conrad was a supporting actor until television made him a star in 'Cannon' in the 1970s.

But in the early 1970s when character-driven detectives who didn't have the look or physique of an action hero were all the rage he found success as an overweight detective who resigns from the Los Angeles Police Department to become a private eye. He uses his knowledge of the system, his contacts in the department and his detective skills to solve many murders and other crimes.

While *Barnaby Jones, Columbo, Ironside, Mannix* and *Quincy M.E.* were doing much the same, Cannon was known for charging high fees to rich clients so that he could help out poorer clients on cases where he charged little or nothing but gave the same dedication to the case.

Quinn Martin Productions

The series was one of Quinn Martin Productions, which was known for its grittier realistic crime in the streets approach to detecting, drama and murder. Shows like *The Streets of San Francisco, Barnaby Jones, Dan August, F.B.I,* and *The Fugitive* were by the same producers. *Cannon*, however was notable because it was the first time a Quinn Martin Production aired on another network other than ABC.

Both *Cannon* and *Barnaby Jones* aired on CBS and crossed over each other at varying times during their network runs. Frank Cannon introduced the Barnaby Jones character, played by Buddy Ebsen, in the third-season episode "Requiem for a Son" in 1973. And in a two-part episode "The Deadly Conspiracy" in 1975 the mystery began on *Cannon* and ended on the follow-up episode of *Barnaby Jones* that aired just after *Cannon* concluded.

In its first season the show built up momentum reaching number 29 in the ratings of all shows that aired during the 1971-72 season. It climbed to 14 for the 1972-73 season and peaked at number 10 for 1973-74. Its later seasons saw a drop as detective dramas overflowed on the networks. In 1974-75 is only reached number 27 and was cancelled in its final season.

Cannon, like many other detective dramas of the day found itself with a plethora of guest stars familiar to TV audiences. Names like Tom Skerritt, Shelley Duvall, David Janssen, Mike Farrell, Sheree North, Martin Sheen, Nick Nolte, Tina Louise, Donna Mills, David Soul, Peter Strauss, Robert Loggia, and Judson Pratt appeared during the series run.

Conrad, however, wasn't done with TV detecting and would return in the 1980s with another successful series that was not far from the character he created in *Cannon*. In fact, many would suggest he simply reprised the character, but had slightly softened with age when *Jake and the Fatman* ran on CBS from 1987 to 1992 with Joe Penny as his sidekick. Conrad was also known for a host of guest appearances on other popular mystery/detective shows like *Murder She Wrote, Matlock, Police Squad* and *Nero Wolfe*.

William Conrad became a familar face to TV audiences for many years. After 'Canon' he would go on to another series 'Jake and the Fatman.'

MURDER on the Boob Tube

MURDER on the Boob Tube

MURDER on the Boob Tube

Charlie's Angels
Detective Drama

First telecast: September 22, 1976
Final telecast: August 19, 1981

Broadcast History:
September 1976-August 1977, ABC Wednesday 10:00-11:00 pm
August 1977-October 1980, ABC Wednesday 9:00-10:00 pm
November 1980-January 1981, ABC Sunday 8:00-9:00 pm
January-February 1981, ABC Saturday 8:00-9:00 pm
June-August 1981, ABC Sunday 8:00-9:00 pm

Cast:
Sabrina Duncan (1976-1979): Kate Jackson
Jill Munroe (1976-1977): Farrah Fawcett-Majors
Kelly Garrett: Jaclyn Smith
Kris Munroe (1977-1981): Cheryl Ladd
Tiffany Welles (1979-1980): Shelly Hack
Julie Rogers (1980-1981): Tanya Roberts
John Bosley: David Doyle
Charlie Townsend: (voice only): John Forsythe

Executive Producer:
Aaron Spelling, Leonard Goldberg

MURDER on the Boob Tube

MURDER on the Boob Tube

Charlie's Angels

Three little girls who went to the police academy

It premiered in September 1976 on ABC Television Network and instantly struck a chord. And it found an audience. Soon, the trio of stars were a sensation. They hit the cover of *Time* Magazine, they had fan clubs, posters, bubble-gum cards, dolls and all the trappings that come with celebrity status. They were *Charlie's Angles*.

But *Charlie's Angels* had a downside. Considered "Jiggle TV" or "T&A TV" (tits and ass), its popularity and acclaim came at a price. No one called it high-brow. There would not be Emmy Awards for acting, writing or directing and the critical acclaim would be in short supply. In fact, its stars would struggle with the desire to prove themselves with meaty or quality acting roles. And those struggles would be played out in the media for all the world to see as several of its stars fought for the right to control their own destinies and distance themselves from TV shows that asked them to go bra-less for ratings.

Charlie's Angels ran on ABC from 1976 to 1981 and was possibly one of the most popular and talked about TV shows of the 1970s. In fact, even today the show seems to be an iconic marker for television of that decade. It was about three women who worked for a private investigation agency and a man named – appropriately enough – "Charlie." He was a man they would never meet in person, but one who would give them their assignments each week via speaker-phone. And off they would go, solving murders, stopping crime and putting the bad guys away. And if they could flip their hair, wear tight-fitting clothes and be as sexy as possible while doing it, all the better.

The show was created by Ivan Goff and Ben Roberts and produced by Aaron Spelling and Leonard Goldberg.

Jaclyn Smith, Farrah Fawcett and Kate Jackson.

Finding Angels

Its first season starred Kate Jackson as Sabrina Duncan, Farrah Fawcett-Majors as Jill Munroe and Jaclyn Smith as Kelly Garrett. But other actresses were considered for roles. Oscar-winning actress Kim Basinger reportedly auditioned for a lead and while she didn't end up as one of the stars she did get cast in one of the episodes during the first season when the angels ended up in a prison break. Other actress considered for one of the leads reportedly were Kathie Lee Gifford and several years later Michelle Pfeiffer auditioned as a replacement for Kate Jackson in the role that eventually went to Shelly Hack.

They were three women who graduated from the police academy in Los Angeles who were uninspired by their duties of working a switchboard or handing out parking tickets. So, they left the force and started working for the Charles Townsend Agency. The office was managed by John Bosley, played by David Doyle, and the angels would inevitably end up going undercover each week on some mysterious, murderous, or dangerous set of assignments that they would have to struggle, fight ... and jiggle ... their way out of.

Initially, the original proposed title for the show was "The Alley Cats," but by the two-hour pilot episode the name had been changed and the three actresses were cast for stardom. Kate Jackson who had already been a familiar face on television in shows including *The Rookies*, was the most notable star, while Smith and Fawcett-Majors were relative newcomers, although Farrah has been doing guest spots in a host of TVs shows back into the late 60s in shows like *I Dream of Jeannie* as well as her then-husband's hit show *The Six Million Dollar Man*. Jaclyn Smith was entering into the show relatively new to acting after being discovered as a model for Breck Shampoo, though she had been doing some small TV spots in shows as far back as 1970 and even some un-credited work prior to that.

MURDER on the Boob Tube

The first season and subsequent seasons tried to mix things up with having the women placed in a variety of different situations. From the roller derby, to women's prison, as well as cases on cruise ships, hospitals, modeling agencies and psychics. Of the show's success Farrah Fawcett-Majors hoped it was talent, but was equally realistic. "When the show was number three [in the ratings], I figured it was our acting" she once said. "When it got to be number one, I decided it could only be because none of us wears a bra."

Fawcett-Majors decided she'd had enough by the end of the first season and quit the show. Many felt she wanted to strike while the iron was hot and move onto bigger things, more money, and better acting roles. However, her contact prevented her from working and it was some time before she would find success beyond the show.

In fact, Fawcett would eventually work out her contractual obligations by returning to the show for a number of guest appearances in seasons three and four.

Changing Faces

For the second season, another newcomer, Cheryl Ladd came aboard as Farrah's character's sister, Kris Munroe and quickly picked up where the show left off as resident blonde beauty. Ladd was a relative newcomer, but had some small roles in TV shows like *The Streets of San*

The original trio became superstars, but the line-up of actresses would change as the series progressed, The series lives on in DVD.

Francisco before being cast as an angel trained in San Francisco.

Kate Jackson exited the show as well at the end of season three in search of better roles as well. Jackson was reportedly in the running for the lead in the feature film *Kramer vs. Kramer*, but when the show's contract prevented her from taking the part Meryl Streep took the part and won a Best Supporting Actress Oscar for her performance. Jackson longed for serious and challenging roles. She was the only angel nominated for an Emmy Award for her acting, though she never won, and was the only Angel to never wear a bathing suit or a bikini during her three seasons on the show.

Jackson was replaced after the fourth season by another model, Shelly Hack, who joined the series as Tiffany Welles from Boston for season four in 1979. After 25 episodes she exited the show at the end of the season and was replaced by the final Angel, Tanya Roberts, who starred alongside Smith and Ladd for season five, the final season of the series in 1980-81.

In its initial season the show ranked number five for the year, but climbed as high as number one. In season two it ranked number four of all shows airing between 1977 and 1978. By season three the show dropped to number 12 and season four it topped out at number 20. By the final season the show had run out of steam.

The Angels had covered just about as much variety the writers could come up with and the change of faces didn't help keep momentum going. It landed barely in the top 60, coming in at number 59 for the final season and the cost of the show most likely signaled its end if the ratings were a sign of where things were headed.

But the network also began shifting the series timeslot in the final two seasons making it more difficult for loyal fans to keep up with the day and time. Moving from 9 pm on Wednesdays to Sundays at 7 pm didn't help and the show also disappeared for a period during the 1981 season entirely between February and June, returning to air the final set of filmed episodes before calling it quits.

Besides Jaclyn Smith, who was the only Angel to last the entire series, David Dolye's Bosely was the only other constant face of the show. The other constant was the voice of Charlie, played unseen by well-known actor John Forsythe. Forsythe would go onto one of his other most famous and visual roles as Blake Carrington shortly after the end of *Charlie's Angels* in another popular ABC series *Dynasty*.

Charlie's Angels would grace the big screen several times with feature films some 20 years later and the original trio of angels would last grace the stage in 2006 for a tribute to their former producer of *Charlie's Angels*, Aaron Spelling shortly after his death. There has also been talk of a new version of the series on TV.

Many of the actresses would go onto further fame with Fawcett and Smith making a name for themselves in several highly successful TV movies. Fawcett would also try her hand at several series including a reality show, *Chasing Farrah*, before her death from cancer in 2009. Smith also appeared in reality TV as host of the series *Shear Genius* and she would launch a successful fashion line. Kate Jackson would return to series television in another successful series, *Scarecrow and Mrs. King* and Cheryl Ladd took up residence in the series *Las Vegas*. Shelly Hack starred in the feature film *The Stepfather* and made guest appearances on TV while Tanya Roberts appeared as a Bond girl in the 007 film *A View to a Kill* and as *Sheena* queen of the jungle as well as TV work in *That 70s Show*.

Shelly Hack, Tanya Roberts and Cheryl Ladd all came in to replace exiting angels showing the series was about the ensemble cast and not a one-star vehicle.

MURDER on the Boob Tube

MURDER on the Boob Tube

MURDER on the Boob Tube

Columbo
Detective Drama

First telecast: September 15, 1971
Final telecast: September 4, 1977

Broadcast History:
September 1971-September 1972 NBC Wednesday 8:30-10:00 pm
September 1972-July 1974, NBC Sunday 8:30-10:00 pm
August 1974-August 1975, NBC Sunday 8:30-10:30 pm
September 1975-September 1976, NBC Sunday 9:00-11:00 pm
October 1976-September 1977, NBC Sunday 8:00-9:30 pm

Cast:
Lt. Columbo: Peter Falk

MURDER on the Boob Tube

MURDER on the Boob Tube

Columbo

Just one more thing ...

Peter Falk is *Columbo*, but it's surprising to many, even those who know the series and the actor well, that he was not the man who gave life to the role.

The *Columbo* character actually first appeared in a 1960 episode of a television-anthology series called *The Chevy Mystery Show*. The episode, entitled "Enough Rope," starred Bert Freed as the would-be detective. He played the character far more traditional that the *Columbo* we've come to know and love. The only similarities were that the detective's suit was rumpled and he smoked a cigar.

MURDER on the Boob Tube

The episode was then transformed into a stage play in 1962 and 70-year-old Thomas Mitchell inhabited the role. While he was much quirkier than the original performance all the famous mannerism were still not in place, but the play, entitled "Prescription Murder" would be the basis of another airing on television. In 1968, a two-hour TV film of *Prescription Murder* was filmed for NBC. But even then, Falk wasn't the network's first choice. Both Bing Crosby and Lee J. Cobb were the first choices. After Crosby turned down the role and Cobb was unavailable director Richard Irving convinced the producers Falk was the man for the job. They wanted an older more seasoned actor and didn't think Falk could pull off the job, but he wanted the part and they gave him a chance.

The movie was considered a pilot for a possible TV series, but the film didn't quite meet the expectations the producers and network had for the show. In part, the *Columbo* character was minimized in the first TV movie since he doesn't appear until more than a half-hour into the film. And the Columbo character was harder-edged and less likeable, so he would be softened in later versions as the series progressed.

While not the first 'Columbo,' Peter Falk would make the role his own and go onto a long as successful career as the rumpled detective.

MURDER on the Boob Tube

It didn't get picked up as a series, but in 1971 the concept was given another shot at life when another pilot was filmed. This time the likeable, rumpled detective came out to catch Lee Grant as a brainy lawyer/murderess who kills her husband in "Ransom for a Deadman." The airing was a hit and the show was picked up as part of the *NBC Mystery Movie*.

Rotating Line-Up

In its first season it aired on Wednesday nights in a rotating line-up alongside other similar-themed hour-and-a-half mysteries. Falk earned an Emmy Award for his work in the first season and the show continued on the network rotating as part of the weekly line-up until 1978. After the first season the series was moved to Sunday nights as part of the Mystery Movie line-up.

The character (who never had a first name), and the series were a creation of the writing/producing team of Richard Levinson and William

Peter Falk would become a TV icon known around the world for his long-running series and collection of tele-films featuring detective Columbo from the late 1960s until 2003. His iconic face would be charatarized on TV Guide.

Link. *Columbo* ran as a television series from 1971 to 1978.

As part of a *Mystery Movie* line-up concept one of three different series was aired on a rotating basis. In addition to *Columbo*, *McMillan & Wife*, starring Rock Hudson and Susan Saint James, and *McCloud* starring Dennis Weaver, made the line-up. Other shows like *Banacek* and *Quincy M.E.* would find their way into American homes via similar rotations. This format suited the producers since the 90-minute stories were more involved and more intricate than the typical hour-long show. At one point the series was even padded out to two-hours between 1974 and 1976 before returning to an hour-and-a-half for the final season.

Quirky Character

Falk's *Columbo* came with a collection of quirks and visual cues that defined his character in what would become a likeable, if not loveable, way. Often chomping on or holding a half-smoked cigar, he was known to drop ashes on the murder victim's floor much to the dismay of those around him. In nearly every episode he appeared in his wrinkled beige raincoat and some witnesses and police took him for a hobo rather than a police detective. He was also known to eat hard-boiled eggs and fried chicken at his crime scenes.

He was also unusual for refusing to carry a weapon. *Columbo* never shot a gun. And his confused manner, which most often was paired forgetfulness, lead to his usual "Just one more thing," request of his murderers. In most cases he seemed as if to pester his murderers to the point they were relieved to finally have it over with so they could head off to prison and away from this annoying yet cunning detective.

The shows themselves veered from the traditional "who-dunnit" as each episode actually started with a murder and a murderer. Turning the classic detective formula upside down, we knew at the very beginning who the victim was and who the killer was, so there, in fact, was no "who-dunnit" for the show. The mystery lay in how the rumpled Columbo would fit the pieces together and uncover and trip up the murderer, once again proving there is no such thing as a perfect murder.

In classic detective dramas murder is by an unknown assailant. The detective arrives on the case, gathering clues and solving the crime for us as viewers. In *Columbo* the killer is placed up front, committing what he or she thinks to be the perfect crime, only to find that the bumbling detective they think they've outwitted is far more savvy than he lets on to be. Even though we see how the murder is planned, committed, and covered we enjoy seeing *Columbo* toy with the killer following the suspect, badgering them with questions and often asking him or her to help solve the very crime they committed.

Many Guest Stars

Columbo was the only regular character in the series, though several supporting detectives were known to appear on and off in the series. There were also countless extras who appeared in bit parts and supporting roles throughout the series that became familiar faces even though they played different characters. And even some of the same killers turned up more than once when actors like Jack Cassidy, Robert Culp, and Patrick McGoohan appeared as killers in several shows. Many other famous guest stars, including Janet Leigh, Vera Miles, William Shatner, Leonard Nimoy, Dick Van Dyke, John Cassavetes, Anne Baxter, Leslie Nielsen, Faye Dunaway, Eddie Albert, John Houseman and others sparred with the detective. Houseman actually murdered in one episode and found him a widow of another victim in another show.

In addition, a cast of young writers, directors, and producers who would go onto greater fame and success got their start or learned their craft through *Columbo* episodes. Steven Spielberg directed a September 1971 episode entitled "Murder by the Book" in what would be the first episode of the series following the pilot. Other notable directors included Jack Smight, Norman Lloyd, and Nicholas Colasanto. Peter Falk even took on the director's role.

On the writers front Stephen J. Cannell (*The Rockford Files, The A-Team, Wiseguy*), Peter S. Fisher (*Murder, She Wrote*), and Steven Bochco (*L. A. Law, Hill Street Blues*) crafted shows during the series. And Dean Hargrove (*Matlock, Perry Mason*) and Roland Kibbee (*Barney Miller*) were producers. Falk also inhabited the executive producer role on numerous occasions and was reportedly earning a hefty $250,000 per show by the end of the series.

In its successful run on television in the 1970s *Columbo* won seven Emmy Awards, including three for Falk and one for the series itself and the show actually launched an ill-fated one spin-off when *Mrs. Columbo* with Kate Mulgrew in the title role ran on NBC in 1979. It was an hour-long series with *Mrs. Columbo* as a reporter solving would-be crimes. But her popular husband never appeared in the show and the series lasted only one season, filming about 13 episodes.

But *Columbo* himself was not gone from the airwaves. After a series of successful TV movies featuring Raymond Burr' as Perry Mason found large audiences in the 80s, Falk returned as the bumbling detective for his own series of *Columbo* TV movies for ABC starting in 1989. The final TV film, "Columbo Likes the Nightlife" aired in January 2003. Since then many of the episodes and films have been re-released on DVD.

MURDER on the Boob Tube

MURDER on the Boob Tube

Dragnet
Police Drama

First telecast: January 3, 1952
Final telecast: September 10, 1970

Broadcast History:
January 1952-December 1955, NBC, Thursday 9:00-9:30 pm
January 1956-September 1958, NBC Thursday 8:30-9:00 pm
September 1958-June 1959, NBC Tuesday 7:30-8:00 pm
July-September 1959, NBC Sunday 8:30-9:00 pm
January 1967-September 1970, NBC 9:30-10:00 pm

Cast:
Sgt. Joe Friday: Jack Webb
Sgt. Ben Romero (1952) Barton Yarborough
Sgt. Ed Jacobs (1952): Barney Phillips
Officer Frank Smith (1952): Herb Ellis
Officer Frank Smith (1953-1959): Ben Alexander
Officer Bill Gannon (1967-1970): Harry Morgan

Director
Jack Webb

Additional Titles:
Dragnet '76, Badge 174, Dragnet '83 and The New Dragnet

MURDER on the Boob Tube

MURDER on the Boob Tube

Dragnet

Just the facts, ma'am

If there were a quintessential detective show that set the bar for all detective shows to come it would be *Dragnet*. First a long-running radio show, it would christen television's crime drama genre and would find itself a staple of television for years to come. It would also find new life in color and syndication as well as on the big screen.

In many ways, even recent detective dramas, from the *Law & Order* variations to the host of *CSI* shows pay homage to *Dragnet*. With focus on a dedicated Los Angeles police detective named Sergeant Joe Friday, and his varying partners, the show was aptly named *Dragnet* after a common term used by police for coordinated measures used in apprehending criminals or suspects. Nearly all detectives shows that followed aimed for creating similar dedicated characters on similar paths to fighting crime and solving murders.

Dragnet was one of the first "real" TV shows that depicted police procedures giving millions of viewers a taste of a world they would hopefully never experience. While the danger and heroism of police work took center stage, it also showed the seedier life of crime and the grueling work of the police. In many ways, the show helped improve public opinion of police officers, even while the real media and news did not.

Actor and producer Jack Webb was the key to the show's success. Webb created the show, produced it and starred in it. Webb actually had a small role as a police forensic scientist in a 1948 film called *He Walked by Night* that proved to be his inspiration for the series. The film was based on the real murder of California Highway Patrol officer in Los Angeles and the idea of a police show based on real stories was what Webb aimed to capture.

Hitting the Airwaves

Originally airing on radio from June 1949 to February 1957 the show hit the television airwaves in December 1951 on NBC and ran until August 1959. After the black and white series ended, the show disappeared from television until 1967 when it found new life in color. NBC

Jack Webb was the creative force behind the concept, creation and long life of 'Dragnet' through the 50, 60s and beyond.

re-launched the series with Web back behind the badge and the show ran from January 1967 until April 1970.

And if all the TV airing was not enough, the show found life in feature film as well. Several times in fact. In 1954 Webb starred in a feature film version that was similar to the version seen on TV and a TV-movie produced in 1966 was the driving force behind the revived color version of the series in the late 1960s. Then in 1987, a comedy that spoofed and honored the show hit theaters. Other revivals on television were attempted in 1989 and again in 2003 and even a comic strip version of show ran in newspapers from 1952 to 1955. Jack Webb even helped write the strip.

"The story you are about to see is true. Only the names have been changed to protect the innocent," marked the opening of each show and Webb aimed to keep the stories as real as possible. He reportedly visited police headquarters, drove on night patrols and attended courses at the police academy to ensure that the cases were told with accuracy.

While there had been other police-type dramas on television when *Dragnet* premiered, none captured the realism or the audience the way Webb's show did. NBC's executives were reportedly not all that in-

Jack Webb was joined by Harry Morgan as his detective partner when the series moved into full color in the late 1960s.

terested but Webb produced a pilot and sought endorsement from the Los Angeles Police Department because he wanted to use cases and investigations from official police files.

Initially, the police were not keen to the idea of real crimes being told on television, but once they obtained assurance that the police would not be depicted unflatteringly and the names would be changed they gave their support. It was this support that would help get the show on the air, but it would also be the point of much of the show's criticism. As the 60s wore on and police practices began to come into question *Dragnet* would find its hands tied in its ability to fairly depict issues surrounding police corruption or the police department's approach to racial segregation policies because of its agreement with police.

Delivering Justice Week to Week

Webb himself narrated the show noting the date and time and activities that took viewers through the story unfolding on screen. And at the end of an episode, announcer Hal Gibney would detail the outcome of the case and fate of the guilty. Suspects were most often tried by a court "in and for the City and County of Los Angeles," and convicted and sent to prison. In some cases they were found mentally incompetent or possibly found guilty and "executed in the lethal gas chamber at the State Penitentiary, San Quentin California."

In rare occasions innocent people were suspected or accused of a crime and even rarer, criminals avoided capture or escaped the justice they had been served. While some such cases found their way into the radio program they were rare on TV. Even so, TV allowed Webb and the show's writers to use real cases from the LAPD's Robbery or Homicide Division. And set designers even used actual details from the division in the show and many of the names of offices in the show came from real officers on the force.

The few fictional names were those of Friday and his partner. Sgt. Ben Romero, played by Barton Yarborough, was Friday's first partner, but when Yarborough died after three episodes he was replaced by Detective Sergeant Ed Jacobs, played by Barney Phillips, and later by Officer Frank Smith, played by Herb Ellis. Ben Alexander took over the role of Officer Smith being one of the few to have a role in both the radio and television version of the show.

When the show ended in 1959 it immediately moved into syndication, but under the name *Badge 714*. It wasn't actually ratings that caused the show to stop, those were reportedly quite good, but Webb himself supposedly wanted to do other things and the syndication offered him the income and presence on TV even if he wasn't filming the show.

1966 Return

Much had changed by the latter part of the 1960s with civil unrest, trouble in the streets and urban cities facing increased dangers from crime. When *Dragnet* came back to network TV it aimed to tell new tales with an even grittier edge. Webb hoped Ben Alexander would reprise his role as well, but he was contracted to another series for ABC called *Felony Squad* and was unable to take part. The part of Friday's partner for the color series was recast and Harry Morgan took the role of Bill Gannon. Morgan would go onto later fame in *MASH*.

A TV movie pilot for the new color series was produced for Universal but actually didn't reach the air until 1969 because NBC quickly debuted the series as a mid-season replacement and put the show into production immediately even without airing the pilot. It was initially named *Dragnet 1967* to differentiate it from the original series. The new series would also distinguish itself by focusing more on story lines centering on troubled youth, drug abuse, and general relations between the police and the community. With other shows like *Mod Squad* on the air as well, *Dragnet*'s aim was to capture an audience of viewers who knew the original show, but also younger viewers who were hip to new trends and expected more modern day approaches to reality.

The show aired for four seasons on NBC with solid ratings and Webb even launched a spin-off spin show called *Adam-12* in 1968 focusing on the lives patrol officers on the beat. *Adam-12* carried on the *Dragnet* brand for seven years even after Webb decided to end *Dragnet* again so he could do other things. Webb would produce another series called *Emergency!*

Another Remake

In 1989, *The New Dragnet* was broadcast in first-run syndication and aimed to recapture the series of the past. It and aired alongside another Webb show, *The New Adam-12*. *The New Dragnet* starred Jeff Osterhage and Bernard White as the detectives, with Don Stroud as the captain. The show lasted three seasons.

It was in 1982 when Webb was in process of bringing *Dragnet* back to television yet again when he suddenly died of a heart attack. *Dragnet '83* reportedly had five scripts completed and a co-star for Webb, Kent McCord, at the time of his death.

But even after Webb's death the franchise continued. In 2003 Dick Wolf, producer of NBC's *Law & Order* franchise, created a show for ABC with Ed O'Neill as Joe Friday. Initially the show stayed close to Webb's original concept but after 12 episodes the series changed to more

While the series took many forms, it was the late 60s version with Jack Webb and Harry Morgan that remains popular with fans.

closely resemble the *Law & Order* series featuring an ensemble cast. *L.A. Dragnet* was the name and in addition to O'Neill, Eva Longoria, who would go onto later fame in *Desperate Housewives*, co-starred alongside Christina Chang, Desmond Harrington and Evan Dexter Parke. With O'Neill's Joe Friday being given less to do the show was canceled after only five new episodes. Additional episodes had been taped and have since aired on cable television. At one point the complete collection was renamed and aired under the name *Murder Investigation* instead of *Dragnet*.

But the original series and color version, both with Webb front and center as Joe Friday, remain a touchstone of television detective shows and it's still finding new audiences today with releases of the series appearing on DVD, allowing new generations to rediscover a TV classic.

MURDER on the Boob Tube

MURDER on the Boob Tube

MURDER on the Boob Tube

MURDER on the Boob Tube

Ellery Queen
Detective Drama

First telecast: March 23, 1975
Final telecast: April 4,1976

Broadcast History:
March 1975-April 1976, NBC Thursdays, 9:00-10:00 pm

Cast:
Ellery Queen: Jim Hutton
Inspector Queen: David Wayne
Frank Flannigan: Ken Swofford
Simon Brimmer: John Hillerman
Sgt. Velie: Tom Reese

Executive Producers:
Richard Levinson and William Link

MURDER on the Boob Tube

MURDER on the Boob Tube

Ellery Queen

The adventures of a great detective

Ellery Queen had been around a long time before he landed on TV in the 1970s. First on radio, *The Adventures of Ellery Queen* ran from 1939 to 1948 as listeners around the country tuned in to imagine him toiling away at the task of solving crimes. And once again, in the 1970s, a series of brief radio spots called the *Ellery Queen's Minute Mysteries* aired with short one-minute cases between radio programs and acted as an advertisement of sorts. The spots had a sponsor and encouraged listeners to solve the mystery and win a prize by calling in. After the case was solved by a listener the mystery is revealed and the sponsor would get the promotion.

A TV Debut

But the character wasn't only familiar as a voice on the radio, From 1950 to 1952 *The Adventures of Ellery Queen* ran on ABC after a brief start on the DuMont Television Network. When Richard Hart, who played Queen, died suddenly, he was replaced by Lee Bowman. The series returned to DuMont in 1954 with Hugh Marlowe as Queen for a brief stint. And finally George Nader took the lead role for *The Further Adventures of Ellery Queen* for the 1958-59 season, but he was replaced by Lee Philips for the last few episodes before the series met its demise.

In 1971, Peter Lawford starred in a television movie entitled *Ellery Queen: Don't Look Behind You*, with veteran actor Harry Morgan playing Inspector Queen, the uncle to Lawford in the TV film.

And then, in 1975 another TV movie aptly called *Ellery Queen* was again aired and the strength of the film was the basis for a new series in 1975 starring Jim Hutton in the title role and David Wayne as his widowed father. The show lasted one season, from 1975-76, but left a mark on mystery fans and detective series lovers and the show is now regarded as a cult classic. Each episode began with the title "The Adventure of …"

Ellery Queen the television series was set in New York City during the late 1940s and each episode offered a "Challenge to the Viewer."

Jim Hutton wasn't the first Ellery Queen, but he would bring the character to life for one season in the 1970s.

Hutton, acting as detective Ellery Queen would step out of the mystery show about 10 minutes before the end of each episode to speak directly with viewers. He would go over the facts of the case inviting viewers to solve the mystery before the big reveal at the conclusion of was show. The series was similar to the radio spots in format, but viewers were not given a chance to call in and win a prize. The break just provided a gimmick of sorts to bring the audience into the show.

There were many celebrity guests during the single season including Milton Berle, Eve Arden, George Burns, Guy Lombardo, Rudy Vallee, Barbara Rush, and Don Ameche.

The Series Debut

The series first aired on NBC in March, 1975 and Hutton's charm was one of the highlights of the show, which was matched only by David Wayne's ornery nature that provided comic relief and warmth with all the gruesome goings-on. The pilot was a 90-minute TV movie that first aired on March 23, 1975. It was then re-run once on September 7, 1975 (the Sunday before the premiere of the series. It was entitled *Too Many Suspects*. When the 60-minute series began that September each had a similar title like *The Adventure of Auld Lang Syne, The Adventure*

Jim Hutton wasnt the only actor to play Ellery Queen, but his 1970s version has become a cult classic with mystery fans.

of the Lover's Leap, The Adventure of the Chinese Dog, The Adventure of the Comic Book Crusader and others.

But ratings never really helped the show achieve the success the network desired and unable to find a large enough audience the series came to an end in April 1976 after about 22 episodes. Airing opposite *The Streets of San Francisco* on ABC and the *Thursday Night Movie* on CBS the series had tough competition. It also had failing situation comedies as a lead-in offering it little help. After its cancellation the series has occasionally seen life in syndication with several airings on A&E Mystery Theatre and The Encore Mystery Channel and Nick At Nite's TV Land.

Jim Hutton died of liver cancer in 1979 at the age of 45 while his costar David Wayne died in 1995 of lung cancer. Hutton's son Timothy would begin acting just about the time his father became ill. The older Hutton saw his son briefly in a TV movie while he was receiving treatment in the hospital.

At one point there were rumors the younger Hutton might reprise his father's most famous character for a TV movie, but the closest he came was as the star of his own mystery series based on another famous detective when Timothy Hutton starred in *A Nero Wolfe Mystery* in 2001-2002. The younger Hutton would win an Oscar for supporting actor in *Ordinary People* a year after his father's death.

Jim Hutton would die of cancer several years after the end of his series, but the show would be the work that he would be most remembered for.

MURDER on the Boob Tube

MURDER on the Boob Tube

MURDER on the Boob Tube

Hart to Hart
Adventure

First telecast: August 25, 1979
Final telecast: July 31, 1984

Broadcast History:
August-October 1979, ABC, Saturday 10:00-11:00 pm
October 1979-July 1984, ABC Tuesday 10:00-11:00 pm

Cast:
Jonathan Hart: Robert Wagner
Jennifer Hart: Stefanie Powers
Max: Lionel Stander

Executive Producer:
Aaron Spelling, Leondard Goldberg

MURDER on the Boob Tube

MURDER on the Boob Tube

Hart to Hart

Their Hobby is ... Murder

William Powell and Myrna Loy delighted audiences as far back as 1934 with the release of *The Thin Man*, a mystery movie featuring Nick and Nora Charles as a wealthy husband and wife duo who use their detective skills to solve a murder. The success of the film lead to a series of follow-up features including *After the Thin Man*, *Another Thin Man* and several other big screen movies. The concept would even turn into a series with Peter Lawford and Phyllis Kirk in the lead roles, but the show only lasted two seasons ending in 1959.

However, *The Thin Man* would be the genesis for a new series that concluded the 1970s and brought style, comedy, drama, mystery and glamour back to the small screen. The show was *Hart to Hart* and the success of the series lies squarely with the talent and chemistry of it stars, Robert Wagner and Stefanie Powers.

ABC played host to *Hart to Hart* as audiences invited Wagner and Powers into their homes each week from 1979 until 1984 to solve murders while living the lap of luxury with their dog Freeway and their butler Max. The series was created by writer Sidney Sheldon and produced by Aaron Spelling and Leonard Goldberg. Spelling and Goldberg had been on a hot streak creating a host of successful shows for ABC including *S.W.A.T., Starsky & Hutch, The Rookies, Charlie's Angels, The Love Boat, Fantasy Island* and more and would go onto create many other shows like *Dynasty, TJ Hooker* and *Vegas*.

Solving Murders and Other Crimes

For *Hart to Hart*, the premise wasn't all that far from *The Thin Man* series, but enough was changed to keep the show from being a total knock-off. Jonathan Hart, played by Wagner, was a self-made million-

Stefanie Powers and Robert Wagner became the dynamic duo for ABC's 'Hart to Hart' television series.

aire and CEO of Hart Industries whose wife Jennifer, played by Stefanie Powers, was a beautiful freelance journalist. As international jetsetters, they lived in a world of mansions, private planes, yachts and glamour that average Americans could only dream about.

In their spare time the couple teamed up as amateur sleuths focused on solving murders, or in some cases other crimes like smuggling, theft, or kidnapping. Lionel Stander portrayed their loyal butler, cook, chauffeur and co-conspirator who often found himself drafted into duty.

The concept for the show reportedly came from novelist and sometimes screenwriter Sidney Sheldon who originally crafted a script for CBS called "Double Twist." The story centered on a married couple who were spies but the script gathered dust until Aaron Spelling and Leonard Goldberg read it and decided an update might make for a successful television series.

The script ended up in the hands of screenwriter Tom Mankiewicz, who had found success writing screenplays for various James Bond features among other projects. Mankiewicz updated the story to make it more contemporary and renamed it *Hart To Hart*. Mankiewicz made his directorial debut filming the two-hour pilot movie and acted as creative consultant for the series after it was picked up by ABC.

Selecting a Young Cary Grant

Spelling and Goldberg's originally imagined Cary Grant in the lead role, but Grant was 75 years old at the time and had long since retired from acting. A younger actor who could channel Grant and bring the same flair and style was needed and Robert Wagner, who female fans referred to as a "dreamy movie star," was selected as the most obvious choice.

For Wagner's onscreen wife Jennifer several actresses including Suzanne Pleshette and Lindsay Wagner, were reportedly considered before Stefanie Powers was selected for her chemistry with Wagner.

A $2 million two-hour pilot movie was filmed. Wagner was recently out of series work after his three-season series *Swtich* was cancelled by CBS, though he was busy at work on other projects like the film *Airport '79* and the miniseries *Pearl*. As for Powers, she had worked with Wagner before on an episode of *It Takes a Thief* in 1970 and he claimed he thought of no one better to portray his onscreen wife.

The show premiered with a TV movie in August 1979 and included a cameo appearance by Wagner's real wife Natalie Wood as Scarlett O'Hara. Wood had partial ownership of the show. The pilot succeeded and the series moved into its first season of hour-long episodes that fall. While the show didn't crack the top 30 in its initial season, by season two it climbed to number 23 in 1980-81. It peaked at number 15 for season three in 1981-82 and leveled off at number 17 for the fourth 1982-83 season. After initial airings of the first season on Saturday night at 10 pm, the show shifted over to Tuesday nights at 10 pm in the fall of 1979 and it would remain in the same timeslot for future seasons allowing fans to keep track and plan to tune in each week.

The Harts were a ratings success after their debut in 1979.

During the run of the series rumors of romance between the stars filled tabloids and gave Wagner's wife reason for jealousy, but the stars claimed no off-screen romance. Tragedy struck in November 1981 when Wagner's wife Natalie Wood drown after falling overboard of their yacht, *Splendour*. Nine days later, when Wagner returned to the set it was Powers who helped him get through filming. He had reportedly also helped her get through the death of companion William Holden after his death during the same period and the work allowed them both to focus on something positive and fans loved the show and the duo.

Cancellation came calling at the close of the fifth season when the series failed to crack the top 30. When it ended the series had produced some 110 television episodes. And over the course of its run the series earned 21 Emmy and Golden Globe nominations It moved into syndication after ending and has since aired in more than 60 countries.

The Characters Resurface

But all was not over for Jonathan and Jennifer Hart when they returned to television in the 1990s for a series of TV movies. In 1993, almost a decade after the series ended, Wagner and Powers starred in *Hart To Hart Returns*.

The success of the reunion movie resulted in a host of new TV movies including *Home Is Where The Hart Is* (1994), *Crimes Of The Hart* (1994) *Old Friends Never Die* (1994), *Secrets Of The Hart* (1995),

The onscreen chemistry of Wagner and Powers lead to rumors of off-screen romance in the newspaper tabloids.

Two Harts In 3/4 Time (1995), and *Harts In High Season* (1996). The final film featuring the duo was *Till Death Us Do Hart* in 1996. Lionel Stander was aboard as Max for five of the movies until his death from lung cancer in 1994. He had completed work on *Secrets Of The Hart*, which aired March 1995.

Since then the show has continued to air in syndication and several seasons have found new audiences on DVD.

MURDER on the Boob Tube

MURDER on the Boob Tube

MURDER on the Boob Tube

Hawaii Five-O
Police Drama

First telecast: September 26, 1968
Final telecast: April 26,1980

Broadcast History:
September-December 1968, CBS Thursday 8:00-9:00 pm
December 1968-September 1971, CBS Wednesday 10:00-11:00 pm
September 1971-September 1974, CBS Tuesday 8:30-9:30 pm
September 1974-September 1975, CBS Tuesday 9:00-10:00 pm
September-November 1975, CBS Friday 9:00-10:00 pm
December 1975-November 1979, CBS Thursday 9:00-10:00 pm
December 1979-January 1980, CBS Tuesday 9:00-10:00 pm
March-April 1980, CBS Saturday 9:00-10:00 pm

Cast:
Det. Steve McGarrett: Jack Lord
Det. Danny Williams (1968-1979): James MacArthur
Det. Chin Ho Kelly(1968-1978): Kam Fong
Det. Kono (1968-1972): Zulu
Gov. Philip Grey: Richard Denning
Det. Ben Kokua (1972-1974): Al Harrington
Coroner Che Fong (1970-1977): Harry Endo
Doc (1970-1976): Al Eban
May (1968-1969): Maggi Parker
Jenny (1969-1976): Peggy Ryan
Attorney General (1968-1969): Morgan White
Attorney General John Manicote (1975-1977): Glenn Cannon
Wo Fat (1968-1975): Khigh Dhiegh
James "Kimo" Carew (1979-1980): William Smith
Truck Kealoha (1979-1980): Moe Keale
Lori Wilson (1979-1980): Sharron Farrell

Additional Title:
McGarrett

MURDER on the Boob Tube

MURDER on the Boob Tube

Hawaii Five-O

Book 'em, Danno

As one of the longest continuous-running detective shows *Hawaii Five-O* stands out not only for its longevity but for its unique landscape and realistic depiction of crime in a tropical paradise. The showed aired from 1968 until 1980, and even with its stark realism Hawaii seemed all the more real and interesting because Steve McGarrett and his band of dedicated officers made it a place we wanted to visit ... if only for an hour each week from our living room couch.

Filmed almost entirely on the Hawaiian Islands, it was a place many Americans had never visited when the show first aired, but the beauty of the landscape and tropical scenery gave the show a different perspective than the traditional New York, Los Angeles, or even San Francisco locales of many other competing detective shows airing at the same time.

But more than that, perhaps the fans gravitated to the strong cast of characters, from the no-nonsense Steve McGarrett to the trusty partner Danny Williams and the cast of locals who added a special charm and authenticity to the goings-on each week. And we can't possibly forget the picturesque title sequence and the theme music that still captivates listeners and makes it instantly recognizable.

It didn't hurt that the show was well written, acted and directed. And as far off as it was it still managed to collect an impressive cast of guest stars over its nearly 12-year run. Helen Hayes, Ricardo Montalban, Leslie Nielsen, Ross Martin, Herbert Lom, Hume Cronyn, Nehemiah Persoff, Ed Flanders, Andrew Duggan, Richard Hatch, John Ritter, Gavin MacLeod, Monte Markham and many more appeared on location.

A Detecting Cast

Jack Lord starred as Steve McGarrett heading up a state police unit that often investigated murder along with organized crime, assassination plots, kidnapping and other forms of crime on the islands. Next to him stood James MacArthur as his handsome and likeable second-in-command Danny – or Danno – Williams. Rounding out the small cast of regulars were local actors Kam Fong, Zulu, Al Harrington, and Herman Wedemeyer.

Created by Leonard Freeman, some sources suggest that Freeman got the idea for the show during or after a conversation with then Governor of Hawaii, John Burns. *Hawaii Five-O* was shot on location in Honolulu, Hawaii, and Oahu. While there was occasional filming in Los Angeles, Singapore and Hong Kong, the Hawaiian islands were front and center in every episode. Others claim Freeman originally wanted to set the series elsewhere but eventually settled on Hawaii. At one time the title for the series was rumored to be *The Man*.

The Original Steve McGarrett

Jack Lord reportedly wasn't even the first choice for McGarrett. Gregory Peck was supposedly offered the role, but turned it down and other actors were considered before Jack Lord was flown to Hawaii and offered the part at the last minute. He reportedly read for the role and was offered the lead on a Wednesday and was in front of the cameras filming the first episode the following Monday.

The biggest challenge for the lead actors and skilled players in the cast and crew was the lack of other seasoned professionals. Crews of skilled technicians for the filming as well as competent supporting or bit-part actors were in short supply and some of the early episodes show the strain under which the series started. Many learned the craft while making the show and some suggest that this even helped the show's longevity as it seemed to get better with time and experience. The show even survived the death of its creator when Freeman died during open heart surgery at the end of the fifth season. The show returned in the fall and lasted another seven years.

Jack Lord would grace the cover of 'TV Guide' numerous times during the show's decade on CBS.

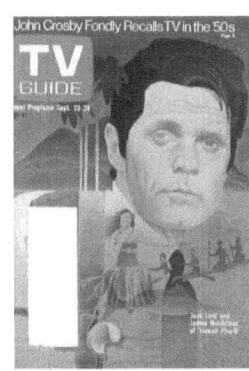

CBS produced the series and it first aired on September 20, 1968. It quickly found an audience and while the *Dragnet's, Columbo's, Cannon's* and *Barnaby Jones'* came and went, *Hawaii Five-O* kept at it, diligently putting the bad guys away until its final episode on April 5, 1980. In fact, the show was on the air so long that reruns of early episodes entered syndication and were running as re-runs as new episodes were still being filmed. The final season, at one point was syndicated under the title *McGarrett*.

As the series progressed many of the faces would change with Lord being the mainstay anchoring the show. Supporting cast members came and went including MacArthur who exited the final season. And for its long run it was even surprising fans stuck with the show as CBS shifted its air date with the series airing on Tuesday, Wednesday, Thursday, Friday and Saturday during its run.

And the series is still airing in syndication today and is reaching whole new audiences with DVD packages.

Over the years there have been a host of rumors, tales and even attempts at re-launching the show as a feature film. Several studios were supposedly interested in the concept and Boston screenwriter George Nolfi was reportedly at work on a script in 2004. One story suggested that it was an old contract that left CBS with the rights to the series that prevented a feature film deal from being worked out. But even after the CBS dispute was reportedly resolved other legal maneuvers from people who owned pieces of the series seems to have prevented a big screen release of the show. There has also been talk of a return with a new version of the show to the small screen. Fans still hope for the day when *Hawaii-Five-O* makes a return.

MURDER on the Boob Tube

MURDER on the Boob Tube

MURDER on the Boob Tube

Ironside
Police Drama

First telecast: September 14, 1967
Final telecast: January 16, 1975

Broadcast History:
September 1967-September 1971, NBC Thursday 8:30-9:30 pm
September-November 1971, NBC Tuesday 7:30-8:30 pm
November 1971-January 1975, NBC Thursday 9:00-10:00 pm

Cast:
Robert T. Ironside: Raymond Burr
Det. Sgt. Ed Brown: Don Galloway
Eve Whitfield (1976-1971): Barbara Anderson
Mark Sanger: Don Mitchell
Fran Belding (1971-1975): Elizabeth Baur
Comm. Dennis Randall: Gene Lyons
Lt. Carl Reese (1969-1975): Johnny Seven
Diana Sanger (1974-1975): Joan Pringle

MURDER on the Boob Tube

Ironside

Even a bullet can't stop this sleuth

Raymond Burr had already conquered television and left an indelible mark in *Perry Mason*, a lawyer who solves the crime, got his client off, and put the bad guy away all in one hour's time. He became an iconic figure who set the bar high for all the television law shows that would follow, much like Jack Webb did for detective shows with *Dragnet*.

However, when *Perry Mason* ended after a nearly 10-year-run on television in 1966 some suggested that no one would ever consider Burr in another role. His portrayal of Mason was so ingrained in the American psyche it would be tough for the actor to find a suitable follow-up. But believe it or not, within a year, Burr was back.

Raymond Burr had been around Hollywood a long time. As an actor he managed to get by much in the same way William Conrad, a fellow murder/detective star did. Both men were of considerable size, and leading man roles were few and far between. But supporting roles as gangsters, cops and sidekicks were much more attainable – certainly, for an actor who could hold his own with a strong performance, but not outshine the luster of the leading man.

Burr would do this best in Alfred Hitchcock's 1954 classic *Rear Window* when he played the wife-killer who stalks James Stewart and Grace Kelly after they discover his dastardly deed. But most of his roles were in smaller B-movies in forgettable films.

TV Makes Him A Star

But *Perry Mason* would change all that and turn Burr into a very successful star. His power in Hollywood and the network's interest in capitalizing on his notoriety and his most famous role meant he could pick and choose the projects he wanted on the small screen, even if his big screen persona was less memorable. But would the public accept him?

In 1967 a TV movie acted as a pilot for the show which introduced Robert T. Ironside to television audiences. It set the stage for the series that would follow as the chief of detectives is shot down while on

Raymond Burr's success on 'Perry Mason' left many suspecting he'd never shed the persona, but roughly a year after the show's end Burr was back with another hit when he starred in 'Ironside.'

vacation. Near death he recovers only to find he is paralyzed from the waste down and confined to a wheel chair. The remainder of the movie has Ironside working his way back into a new career as a special consultant to the San Francisco Police Department, pulling together a small team of detectives to assist him and embarking on a case to find out who crippled him.

A veteran of more than 20 years of police service, Ironside is a grumpy, loud, decisive man who takes some getting used to. He houses himself in the attic of the SFPD headquarters where he lives and works and obtains a specially-modified police truck and later a van to transport himself around town with help from his small team. The show's success came purely from Burr's strong performance as a man who's disability left him dependent on his brains, intuition and guts to solve the crime and bring the criminals to justice.

Supporting Burr was Don Galloway who portrayed Detective Sgt. Ed Brown and acted as a pair of strong legs for Chief Ironside. In addition, a young rich society girl who fancies herself as plainclothes police officer named Eve Whitfield was played by Barbara Anderson. Both assisted Chief Ironside in his cases doing much of the dirty work as he wheels himself into place for the arrest. An assistant/chauffeur named Mark Sanger played by Don Mitchell, also takes on a key role alongside Ironside. Sanger eventually becomes a lawyer by the end of the series. The only other regular was Commissioner Randall, Ironside's friend and boss played by Gene Lyons.

Casting Changes

By the fourth season, Barbara Anderson left the show over a reported contract dispute and was replaced by another young policewoman named Fran Belding, played by Elizabeth Baur. Baur would remain through the remainder of the series until it ended in 1975 when ratings were declining and audiences were more interested in a new brand of detective show. *The Streets of San Francisco* was a similar series also set in San Francisco but filmed entirely on location in San Francisco and had grittier and edgier stories and a more youthful attitude. The show, among others, made *Ironside* seem a bit dated as the series wore on.

After its cancellation the show would remain popular in reruns when it went into syndication. And it was this popularity, along with the host of detective revivals in the 1990s that lead to a reunion show, *The Return of Ironside*, in 1993. The movie aired shortly before Burr's death in September of the same year. Burr had been busy finding similar success with a series of *Perry Mason* reunion TV movies.

As one of the longer-running police dramas of the 60s and 70s, *Ironside* had more than its share of special guest stars. Many of the names would go onto bigger fame and notable actors included Randolph Mantooth, Sharon Gless, Bernie Kopell, Frank Gorshin, Pernell Roberts, E.G. Marshall, Harrison Ford, John Schuck, Susan Saint James,

The cast of 'Ironside.'

Pat Hingle, Anne Francis, David Carradine, Charo, Joseph Campanella, Alan Hale Jr., Marion Ross, Marcia Strassman, Susan Sullivan, Suzanne Pleshette, Bo Hopkins, David Cassidy, Tina Louise, Joel Grey, and Bruce Lee, among others.

In 1971, Burr, Mitchell and Galloway all in their *Ironside* characters took on roles as guest stars in a TV pilot for the series starring George Kennedy called *Sarge*, but the series didn't have the same longevity and only lasted one season airing 14 episodes.

While the original series took place in San Francisco, little of the show was actually filmed there with some early location filming of the actors in popular locations and the footage would be added to episodes throughout the season. For the reunion movie, the story takes place in Denver where the Ed Brown character has supposedly been made deputy police chief. It would mark one of the final appearances of Raymond Burr.

'Ironside' and Raymond Burr shed new light on the challenges of people with disabilities and the show was one of the first with a disabled man as the lead character.

MURDER on the Boob Tube

MURDER on the Boob Tube

MURDER on the Boob Tube

Mannix
Detective Drama

First telecast: September 16, 1967
Final telecast: August 27, 1975

Broadcast History:
September 1967-September 1971, CBS Saturday10:00-11:00 pm
September 1971- September 1972, CBS Wednesday 10:00-11:00 pm
September-December 1972, CBS Sunday 9:30-10:30 pm
January 1973-September 1974, CBS Sunday 8:30-9:30 pm
September 1974-June 1975, CBS Sunday 9:30-10:30 pm
July-August 1975, CBS Wednesday 10:00-11:00 pm

Cast:
Joe Mannix: Mike Conners
Lou Wickersham (1967-1968): Joseph Campanella
Peggy Fair (1968-1975): Gail Fisher
Lt. Adam Tobias (1969-1975): Robert Reed

MURDER on the Boob Tube

Mannix

The name's Mannix, my friend ... Joe Mannix

He was the quintessential private eye. He was a loner, could hold up his end of a fight and, like a dog with a bone, he refused to give up until he got his man ... or woman. He was Joe Mannix, better known to television audiences simply as *Mannix*.

It first aired in September 1967 on CBS. Filmed on the same lot as *Mission Impossible* and using some of the same sets, the series aired for eight seasons, until the spring of 1975. While *Mission Impossible* kicked off in 1966, a season before *Mannix*, it ended in 1973, two seasons before *Mannix* closed his doors with *Mannix* outlasting his brother series by a season.

The show started off on one path, but changed courses after the first season and never strayed much after that. During season one Joe Mannix was employed by Intertect, a big Los Angeles detective agency. And at one point, the story goes, the title of the show was proposed as *Intertect*. Fortunately the name was changed to the surname of the title character and after one season the format was changed and Intertect no longer employed Joe Mannix when season two premiered.

With less than spectacular ratings in season one, the changes were hoped to bring new live to the fledgling series. Mike Conners remained as the star of the show, but Joseph Campanella, who played his boss in season one, was gone and *Mannix* was on his own, running his own agency with the help of a dedicated secretary named Peggy, played by Gail Fisher.

The production company for *Mannix* was Desilu, which was owned by Lucille Ball. The producer of the series was Bruce Geller, who was better known for his hit *Mission Impossible*.

Conners was reportedly cast after he was spotted by Gary Morton driving around Hollywood in a 1937 Bentley convertible. Conners had been known mostly for his film work which included starring opposite Joan Crawford and Jack Palance in *Sudden Fear* and opposite Bette Davis and Susan Hayward in *Where Has Love Gone?* among other features. Morton, according to one story, was a car buff and Lucille Ball's

Mike Conners was Joe Mannix from the late 1960s through much of the 1970s on CBS.

husband and during his conversation with Conners about his car Morton recalled his wife's studio was looking for a detective for a new TV series and felt Conners would be perfect.

A Regular Joe

Joe Mannix came across as a regular "Joe" so to speak. He didn't mince words and often found himself right in the middle of the gunfire, fist fights and brawls. In fact, Mannix may have been shot, knocked out and beaten up more than any other crime fighting detective to ever hit the airwaves.

During the run of the show *Mannix* was shot at least a dozen times and knocked unconscious in what seemed like every episode. He lived and worked at 17 Paseo Verdes West Los Angeles and went into the private eye business after a stint in the Korean War. According to show trivia he got his private investigator license in 1956.

The series was notable for its use of blocked split-screens during the opening credits. It was a sequence similarly used in feature films at the time like *The Thomas Crown Affair*. The show would utilize the imagery between commercial breaks as well.

A Popular Star and Show

Mike Connors popularity would help keep the show on the network against stiff competition from many other similar detective dramas. He was nominated four times for Golden Globe Awards, and won his only one in 1970. He was also nominated for four Emmy Awards. His co-star Gail Fisher was also nominated for four Emmy Awards, winning once also in 1970. She won two Golden Globe Awards in three nominations.

The series was nominated twice as Best Dramatic Series but lost the Emmy Award both times, and had four nominations for Golden Globe Awards as best series, winning the award in 1972.

The series would air in a host of timeslots during its run, but fans seemed to stick with the show no matter what the time or day was until the final season when the show ended in August of 1975.

Conners returned to the role he made famous in 1993 for a special episode of the Dick Van Dyke detective series *Diagnosis Murder*. The showed featured an unsolved *Mannix* case and use flashbacks of the original series along with present day Mannix back on the case. And many years later, during its years in syndication, Mike Conners was awarded a TV Land Award in 2003 as Favorite Crime Stopper in Drama. DVD releases of several seasons have engaged new audiences as well to rediscover the classic series.

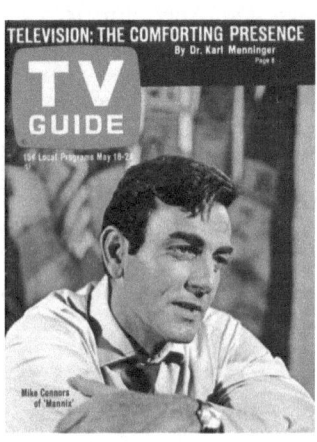

Mike Conners had success on the big screen, but found his greatest fame for his role as the lone detective in 'Mannix.'

MURDER on the Boob Tube

MURDER on the Boob Tube

MURDER on the Boob Tube

McCloud
Police Drama

First telecast: September 16, 1970
Final telecast: August 28, 1977

Broadcast History:
September-October 1970, NBC Wednesday 9:00-10:00 pm
March - August 1971, NBC Wednesday 9:00-10:00 pm
September 1971 - August 1972, NBC Wednesday 8:30-10:00 pm
September 1972 - August 1975, NBC Sunday 8:30-10:00 pm
September 1975-August 1976, NBC Sunday 9:00-11:00 pm
October 1976-August 1977, NBC Sunday various

Cast:
Sam McCloud: Dennis Weaver
Peter B. Clifford: J.D. Cannon
Sgt. Joe Broadhurst: Terry Carter
Chris Cough.in: Diana Muldaur
Sgt. Grover: Ken Lynch

MURDER on the Boob Tube

MURDER on the Boob Tube

McCloud

A fish out of water

NBC had what they thought would be a winning concept – and they were right. They created a "series" around the concept of tying together telefilms that shared a common theme – murder, and they aired them each week in a rotating fashion. The concept quickly caught on and they had a band of shows sharing a timeslot and a set of loyal viewers. But they key would always be in ensuring that the shows held enough commonality to capture an audience week after week, but deliver enough uniqueness that the shows stood on their own.

The key to success of the shows would rely most heavily on the characters that anchored each show. While the murders came and went and the detecting, the clues, the suspects and the victims often held similarities, the title characters would have to be independent, quirky and enjoyable to watch, keeping us on the edge of our seats and returning week after week. But the leads would be different enough from one another to give them a unique flavor.

While Lieutenant Columbo was most often disheveled, confused and forgetful, and Commissioner McMillan was well-read, thoughtful, bold and handsome, the third wheel in the trio had to somehow bring a special brand of detective to the small screen. A cowboy in New York City whose homespun wisdom, keen sensibilities and backwoods approach kept his cohorts on edge and offered viewers something they hadn't seen on television. *McCloud* was the show.

McCloud premiered on February 17, 1970 with Dennis Weaver in the title role as Marshal Sam McCloud. In the pilot film he was an officer from Taos, New Mexico who gets caught up in mystery and intrigue when he escorts a prisoner from New Mexico to New York. "Portrait of a Dead Girl" was the name of the episode and after McCloud solves the complicated murder case he is put on semi-permanent "special assignment" with the New York City Police Department solving unusual or high-profile crimes.

The theme was loosely lifted from a 1968 Clint Eastwood film called *Coogan's Bluff* and one of the familiar sights that both shared was

Dennis Weaver starred as 'McCloud' on NBC.

the image of a masculine cowboy on horseback in the middle of a busy New York street full of people, cars, taxis and public transit.

Part of a Trio of Shows

The pilot worked and NBC picked up the show and quickly put into the line-up rotating it first in 60-minute episodes on Wednesday nights with three other shows, *Night Gallery, San Francisco International Airport* and *The Psychiatrist*. It did well enough in the first season to get picked up for return. While *McCloud* reportedly came in at number 19 on the Nielsen ratings, its counterparts didn't fair as well and for the 1971-72 season *McCloud* was extended to 90 minutes, airing from 8:30 to 10 p.m. as part of the Mystery Movie series rotating with new shows *Columbo* and *McMillan & Wife*.

The trio was a hit, reaching 14 in the ratings for the year, and with two new murder mysteries debuting *McCloud* was the old favorite to help draw in viewers who stuck with the show from season one. All three shows were then moved from Wednesday to Sunday night where they became a staple of Sunday night television. *McCloud* aired on NBC from 1970 to 1977.

By the fifth season the shows were extended to two hours, but by 1975 they were back again at 90 minutes where they remained for the sixth and seventh seasons. *McCloud*'s final season, 1976-77 lasted until

'McCloud on 'TV Guide.'

April 1977 when the final episode "McCloud Meets Dracula" was aired. A total of 46 shows had been produced in total by the time the series came to a close.

Dennis Weaver was pivotal to the show's success and received Emmy nominations in both 1974 and 1975 as Outstanding Lead Actor in a Limited Series.

McCloud moved into syndication after ending its run, but in 1989, Dennis Weaver reprised *McCloud* in a television movie entitled *The Return of Sam McCloud*. By now, *McCloud* was a senator from New Mexico who ends up embroiled in a new mystery. Today, the show still lives on in DVD.

MURDER on the Boob Tube

MURDER on the Boob Tube

McMillan & Wife
Police Drama

First telecast: September 29, 1971
Final telecast: August 21, 1977

Broadcast History:
September 1971-August 1972, NBC Wednesday 8:30-10:00 pm
September 1972-July 1974, NBC Sunday 8:30-10:00 pm
September 1974-July 1975, NBC Sunday 8:30-10:00 pm
September 1975-August 1976, NBC Sunday 9:00-11:00 pm
December 1976-August 1977, NBC Sunday 8:00-9:30 pm

Cast:
Stuart McMillan: Rock Hudson
Sally McMillan (1971-1976): Susan Saint James
Sgt. Charles Enright: John Shuck
Mildred (1971-1976): Nancy Walker
Agatha (1976-1977): Martha Raye
Stg. Steve DiMaggio: (1976-1977): Richard Gilliland
Maggie (1976-1977): Gloria Strook

Other Name:
McMillan (final season)

MURDER on the Boob Tube

McMillan & Wife

A dynamic duo on the hunt of murderers

If *Columbo* and *McCloud* were lone detectives finding their way through murder and mayhem all by themselves, Stewart McMillan differentiated himself by having a lovely but kooky wife at his side and a lovable housekeeper to keep things light.

McMillan & Wife was considered a light-hearted crime drama series when it debuted on September 17, 1971 as part of a rotating *NBC Mystery Movie*. On Wednesday evenings during the first season, the show starred Rock Hudson and Susan Saint James as the title characters. In 90-minute TV films, the series shared its timeslot in rotation with *Columbo* and *McCloud*. After one season on Wednesday nights, all three mystery shows relocated to Sunday nights where they remained until 1977. The 1975-76 season was extended to two hours, but when it returned for the final season it would be back to its usual hour-and-a-half time frame but with some changes.

Stewart McMillan, played by Rock Hudson, was the commissioner of police in San Francisco, who, along with his young attractive wife Sally, played by Susan Saint James, found themselves often embroiled in murder mysteries that usually related to McMillan's police work.

Quirky Cast of Characters

What made *McMillan & Wife* special wasn't just that the couple shared screen time solving crimes, but that they shared it with a collection of quirky characters equally fascinating and fun to watch. John Schuck, as Sgt. Charles Enright, found himself often acting as McMillan's partner and back-up, while Nancy Walker as the couple's housekeeper Mildred, proved central to the show's success with comic relief against the backdrop of murder. In addition, the show had its share of celebrities guests mixing things up, including Martha Raye, Donna Mills, Andrew Duggan, Michael Ansara, Vito Scotti, Jackie Coogan, Carol Cook, Gordon Jump, John Astin, Stefanie Powers, William Windom and more.

Star of the series, Rock Hudson was comfortable in the spotlight

Susan Saint James and Rock Hudson created onscreen chemisty as 'McMillan & Wife' on NBC.

and the star of major motions pictures like *Giant, Pillow Talk, Written on the Wind, Seconds, Ice Station Zebra* and countless others. But in *McMillan & Wife* he seemed to enjoy sharing the screen time and lessening his workload. While work in a full-time series could be exhausting and all-encompassing, sharing the time on screen allowed him to remain the star of the show but take part in a much more ensemble cast which helped the show gel and find a unique rhythm many other detective shows of the time didn't share. In fact, decades later many crime dramas, from *CSI* to *Law & Order, Cold Case* and others have ensemble casts that balance and unite the show.

Reportedly contract negotiations between Susan Saint James and the show's producers fell apart during the fifth season and the actress exited the show. To explain the absence of McMillan's wife, the writers chose to killer her off along with their unseen son in a plane crash.

When the series returned for the sixth and final season it had been renamed simply *McMillan* with Rock Hudson remaining in the title role but without his ensemble band from previous years. Nancy Walker left for her own series and was replaced my Martha Raye and *McMillan* moved from his large home into an apartment. The show aired about 15

The Stuart McMillans on TV Guide in the 1970s.

episodes during the 1976-77 season and ended its run on April 24, 1977.

Unlike most of his fellow detectives *McMillan* never returned to the small screen. While *Perry Mason, Columbo, Ironside, Mannix, McCloud* and others would reprise their famous detective roles, Rock Hudson hung up the role and moved onto other things including feature films and several other TV shows, including *The Devlin Connection* in 1982 and *Dynasty* from 1984-1985. When Husdon died in July 1985 Stuart McMillan died with him although the series lives on in DVD.

For the final season the series was retitled 'McMillan' after Saint James exited the show and her character was written out of the series.

MURDER on the Boob Tube

MURDER on the Boob Tube

MURDER on the Boob Tube

Perry Mason
Law Drama

First telecast: September 21, 1957
Final telecast: January 27, 1974

Broadcast History:
September 1957-September 1962, CBS Saturday 7:30-8:30 pm
September 1962-September 1963, CBS Thursday 8:00-9:00 pm
September 1963-September 1964, CBS Thursday 9:00-10:00 pm
September 1964-September 1965, CBS Thursday 8:00-9:00 pm
September 1965-September 1966, CBS Sunday 9:00-10:00 pm
September 1973-January 1974, CBS Sunday 7:30-8:30 pm

Cast:
Perry Mason: Raymond Burr
Della Street: Barbara Hale
Paul Drake: William Hopper
Hamilton Burger: William Talman
Lt. Arthur Tragg (1957-1965): Ray Collins
David Gideon (1960-1962): Karl Held
Lt. Anderson (1961-1965): Wesley Lau
Lt. Steve Drumm (1965-1966): Richard Anderson
Sgt. Brice (1965-1966): Lee Miller
Terrence Clay (1965-1966): Dan Tobin

Cast of The New Perry Mason (1973-1974)
Perry Mason: Monte Markham
Della Street: Sharon Acker
Paul Drake: Albert Stratton
Lt. Arthur Tragg: Dane Clark
Hamilton Burger: Harry Guardino
Gertrude Lade: Brett Somers

Created by:
Erle Stanley Gardner

MURDER on the Boob Tube

Perry Mason

It was a case of murder

It wasn't a detective drama, but murder was nearly always at the core of *Perry Mason*. One of the longest running TV shows in history, *Perry Mason* ran from 1957 until 1966 and would make a grand return decades later.

Played by Raymond Burr, Perry Mason was a defense attorney in Los Angeles who almost never lost a case. It is perhaps the best known and most successful law series to ever hit the air and was originally based on a successful series of novels by Erle Stanley Gardner that began in the 1930s.

MURDER on the Boob Tube

A Format the Worked

While the show was quite predictable it was the finesse with which Burr built the case, uncovered the murderer and brought justice all in less than an hour that had viewers tuning in week after week. Along with his dedicated assistant Della Street, Mason would often find himself up against insurmountable odds as the first half of the show set the story in motion when an often-deserving victim is found murdered and Perry's client is usually heard making wild accusations like "I'm gonna kill you," shortly before the crime.

Perry's investigator Paul Drake is almost always on hand for helping discover the body and any clues that might be present and it's usually up to Perry Mason to put the pieces of the puzzle together before his client is sent off to prison or worse. The conclusion of the show often has Mason in the courtroom reenacting the crime or demonstrating how impossible it would be for his client to commit the murder and then unveiling who the real killer is. The murderer often then breaks down or gives in under exhaustion and confesses to the crime. Sometimes the killer was discovered before the trial ever hit the courtroom, but the tale

Raymond Burr found stardom as 'Perry Mason' in the 1950s.

most often unfolded about the same. District Attorney Hamilton Burger would act as Perry's nemesis in most of the series, bent on a guilty verdict at almost all costs. It wasn't so much that Burger was a bad guy, but rather he was blinded by the need for justice and always convinced that the police had arrested the right killer.

Barbara Hale was an RKO actress who was mostly in forgettable B-movies until *Perry Mason* turned her into a star and William Hopper played detective Paul Drake. William Talman played Burger, but as the show went on various co-stars came and went, though Hale stood by Perry through it all.

The series always did well in the ratings no matter who it was up against. And as the years wore on Burr tired of the role and often threatened each season would be his last. But the money and the fame were hard to give up. Once an average supporting actor, Burr never had the looks or physique of a leading man and it wasn't until he landed on television that he became a star.

The show was so successful that the producers found themselves often willing to cater to Burr's demands and the show couldn't really go on without him. *Perry Mason* made Raymond Burr a very rich man and a bankable commodity in Hollywood.

When the series finally ended in 1966 many thought Burr would never escape the character that had made him so famous, but he returned with a new show about a year later and audiences once again gravitated to the actor in *Ironside*.

Perry Mason would make a return to the small screen in the

Raymond Burr had been successful in films but rarely as the star. He most often played supporting roles until television made him a household name.

1970s when Monte Markham inhabited the role for one season during 1973-74. *The New Perry Mason* debuted in September 16, 1973 but without Raymond Burr at the helm the show never seemed to find its audience and was cancelled after 15 episodes in January 1974. But television was not done with *Perry Mason*.

A Return of Mason

Beginning in 1985 Raymond Burr and Barbara Hale reattached themselves to the roles of Perry Mason and Della Street for a very successful run on television in some 30 TV movies featuring Perry Mason back on the case. William Katt and later William R. Moses took up residence as Perry's investigator for the films. From 1985 until Burr's death in 1993 the cast took part in a series of successful TV films.

While CBS was home to the original long-running series, it was NBC that made the lucrative decision to bring Mason back to the small screen and the TV movies were a huge hit. In many ways it was the return of *Perry Mason* that launched a revival of old-time TV detectives and the 1990s saw many old classics dusted off for telefilms, though none with the success and longevity of *Perry Mason*. Even after Burr's death three follow up films that had been in production with the intention of starring Burr were filmed and aired. Each title started with "A Perry Mason Mystery" and starred Hal Holbrook who, as another lawyer, filled in during "Perry's absence," but the story remained basically the same.

Perry Mason, now on DVD and syndication, is still finding new viewers.

MURDER on the Boob Tube

MURDER on the Boob Tube

MURDER on the Boob Tube

Quincy, M.E.
Medical Detective Drama

First telecast: October 3, 1976
Final telecast: September 4, 1983

Broadcast History:
October 1976-January 1977, NBC Sunday 8:00-9:30 pm
Feburary 1977-March 1978, NBC Friday 10:00-11:00 pm
September 1978-April 1980, NBC Thursday 9:00-10:00 pm
September 1980-September 1983, NBC Wednesday 10:00-11:00 pm

Cast:
Quincy: Jack Klugman
Sam Fujiyama: Robert Ito
Dr. Astin: John S. Ragin
Lt. Frank Monahan: Garry Walberg
Stg. Brill: Joseph Roman
Danny Tovo: Val Bisoglio
Lee (1976-1977): Lynette Mettey
Ed: Eddie Garrett
Bartender (1977-1983): John Nolan
Dr. Emily Hanover (1979-1983): Anita Gillette

MURDER on the Boob Tube

MURDER on the Boob Tube

Quincy, M.E.

I see dead people ... and they was murdered!

J ack Klugman was an unlikely actor to be cast as an unconventional crime-buster. While certainly not unknown to television viewers after having appeared in countless shows as far back as the early 1950s, Klugman was also known for some big screen appearances as well.

With shows like *Alfred Hitchcock Presents, The Philco Television Playhouse, Gunsmoke* and *General Electric Theater* under his belt he was also known to moviegoers for noteworthy films like *Twelve Angry Men, Days of Wine and Roses, I Could Go on Singing* and *Goodbye Columbus* that found him in mainstream pictures as a supporting actor with bigger stars overshadowing him. But it was always the small screen that left him destined for stardom.

Success on the Small Screen

His biggest success came after *The Odd Couple*, a Neil Simon play that became a hit movie in 1968 with Walter Matthau and Jack Lemmon, was selected for TV as a half-hour situation comedy. From September 1970 until March 1975 Klugman delighted audiences as the gruff and messy Oscar Madison to Tony Randall's anal-retentive and neat-freak Felix Unger. The show became an instant classic and earned Klugman Emmy nominations for each of its five season, with him winning two awards as Best Actor in a Comedy Series.

With success like that Klugman was welcome at almost any network, but as a comedy star. It seemed unlikely he'd make much of drama, even though he had the history to prove it. But with a movie role in the action packed *Two-Minute Warning* in 1976, a film about sniper at a major league football stadium, he still had adventure and excitement in his blood.

Just before the movie hit the big screen though, Klugman debuted on NBC in a new TV series that was a far cry from his work on *The Odd Couple*. The show was *Quincy, M.E.*. The actor once said in

Jack Klugman found TV fame in comedy when he starred in 'The Odd Couple' before he went onto star as Quincy, M.E.

an interview he wasn't even sure he wanted to do the series, but his wife talked him into it.

A Show on Rotation

Produced at Universal Studios and airing on NBC, *Quincy, M.E.* landed on television on October 3, 1976, as a series of 90-minute telefilms intended as part of the network's long-running Sunday Mystery Movie. The show's extended format allowed it to move into rotation alongside a series of similar shows featuring the same time slot and equal amounts of murder and intrigue.

Columbo, McCloud and *McMillan* were heading into their final seasons and NBC was possibly looking for a way to freshen up or relaunch the franchise. However the initial season only lasted four episodes though as the Mystery Movie format came to a close, but *Quincy, M.E.'s* success was strong enough to earn renewal from the network for a second shot.

Klugman starred in the title role as a Los Angeles County medical examiner whose cases often involve murder and his stepping out of the role of coroner and into the role of detective to solve the crime and bring the killer to justice.

Shortly after the end of the mystery movie series, *Quincy, M.E.* debuted a second season in February 1977 in a new hour-long format. The first show was actually a two-part episode, possibly a hangover from the 90-minute format, but the later shows followed a one-hour format with the murder and investigation leading the good coroner usually into danger until the police showed up to help clean up the mess.

Quincy lived on a houseboat and although popular with the ladies, he was pretty much married to his work. His co-conspirator was his sidekick Sam Fujiyama, played by Robert Ito, who helped in the lab often discovering forensic clues that would assist Quincy in solving the crime, though his character rarely left the lab.

Lots of Guest Stars

Like most good detective shows, *Quincy, M.E.* has his share of celebrity guest stars, including Joseph Campanella, Diana Muldaur, Tyne Daly, June Lockhart, Robert Alda, Gerald S. O'Loughlin, Carolyn Jones, William Daniels, John Ireland, Sam Groom, Ed Begley Jr., Buddy Hackett and more.

The series held out for eight seasons, ending in the fall of 1983. It was nominated for 10 Emmy Awards during its run, including several for Klugman as Outstanding Lead Actor, but he never won for the show. The series was novel in that few shows on television explored forensic science. In the 1970s, the scientific aspect to solving crime was always less intriguing than the detective side of things. But the success of Klugman's series would lead to many other shows centering on the science of crime. Reality shows like *Forensic Detectives* as well as the *C.S.I.* franchise prove that science can sell a murder for TV audiences. A recent count of TV shows found that some 35 to 40 shows on a recent week of TV centered on the topic of forensic science.

Unlike many of his crime-stopping counterparts, Jack Klugman never returned to the role he made famous, although he did reprise his role in *The Odd Couple* for a TV movie in 1993. He did however come close when he starred in two episodes of Dick Van Dyke's *Diagnosis Murder* in 1997 and 1999 and playing a doctor in an episode of *Crossing Jordan* in 2002. Klugman was diagnosed with throat cancer in 1989 and

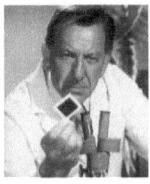

'Quicy, M.E.' was one of the first murder shows to focus on the forensic science behind the crime.

lost a vocal chord to the disease. He recovered but the loss left him with a raspy voice but didn't take away his desire for performing.

A Lawsuit Lingers

But Klugman's association with *Quincy, M.E.* didn't end in 1983. Some 25 years later Klugman filed a lawsuit against NBC for profits he claimed he never received for the series. Reportedly the actor's 1976 contract with the network stipulated that his production company, Sweater Productions, should have received 25 percent of the show's net profits during its run and later syndication. Klugman, however, didn't actually have a copy of his contact because he claimed it was lost after his agent's death and NBC refused to provide a copy.

The lawsuit was an attempt to force NBC to show Klugman the contract and pay him profits he felt he was due. Klugman tolled the Associated press, "I recently heard that they made $250 million and it's still on TV in Germany. I don't want their money. I want my money,"

NBC refused to respond to the lawsuit but reportedly provided Klugman with an accounting statement that showing the series lost money – some $66 million through 2006. In the summer of 2008 the actor reportedly won the right to see his NBC contract. Klugman said "I worked my tail off. I got up at four in the morning and stayed at the studio. I did rewrites, I edited."

Quincy, M.E. is now on DVD finding new audiences.

MURDER on the Boob Tube

MURDER on the Boob Tube

MURDER on the Boob Tube

MURDER on the Boob Tube

The Streets of San Francisco
Police Drama

First telecast: September 16, 1972
Final telecast: June 9, 1977

Broadcast History:
September 1972-April 1973, ABC Saturday 9:00-10:00 pm
September 1973-March 1974, ABC Thursday 10:00-11:00 pm
September 1974-March 1976, ABC Thursday 9:00-10:00 pm
September 1976-June 1977, ABC Thursday 10:00-11:00 pm

Cast:
Lt. Mike Stone: Karl Malden
Det. Steve Keller (1972-1976): Michael Douglas
Jeannie Stone (1973-1976): Darleen Carr
Inspector Dan Robbins (1976-1977): Richard Hatch

Executive Producer:
Quinn Martin

MURDER on the Boob Tube

MURDER on the Boob Tube

Streets of San Francisco

A Quinn Martin production

Over the years there have been numerous television shows set in San Francisco. With its picturesque views and scenic locales, the city by the bay provides an excellent backdrop regardless of whether it's drama, comedy, crime or adventure. But few shows made the city a supporting cast member in the way that *The Streets of San Francisco* did.

From the first airing on September 16, 1972 until the end on June 9, 1977, the ABC series acted as a showcase for the actors as well as the city. It was produced by Quinn Martin Productions, producer of numerous crime show like *The F.B.I., Dan August, Cannon* and *Barnaby Jones* and it quickly found an audience of loyal viewers looking for something different.

When the show first aired it was a risky proposition. Debuting on Saturday evenings at 9 p.m. it was up against some formidable competition. *Mary Tyler Moore* and *The Bob Newhart Show* were staples of Saturday night airing in the same timeslot on CBS. It was a risky shot of counter-programming by ABC, but the risk paid off.

Airing just after another new series, *The Rookies*, it didn't even have any help of a lead in show to pull viewers. *The Rookies* had reportedly debuted less than a week earlier and still hadn't established a following, but even against the odds *The Streets of San Francisco* earned high marks for realism and its gritty portrayal of a pair of dedicated detectives fighting an uphill battle against crime in a major metropolitan city.

A Dynamic Duo

Unlike a lot of detective shows on the air, *The Streets of San Francisco* had a pair of detectives, each strong and with a distinct personality. And the banter and relationship, as well as the chemistry between the two, was what made the show work. The series was based on a detective novel by Carolyn Weston named *Poor, Poor Ophelia*.

Karl Malden, a well-known film actor with supporting roles in

Filmed almost entirely on location in San Francisco, Karl Malden and Michael Douglas starred in the hit series often with cable cars and the Golden Gate Bridge or other sites in the background.

classics like *I Confess, On the Waterfront, Fear Strikes Out, A Streetcar Named Desire, Gypsy, Pollyanna*, and many others was the initial star of the series. But Michael Douglas, a newcomer to the world of television had acting in his blood. The son of actor and movie star Kirk Douglas, the young actor had impressive shoes to fill, but the instincts and charisma to do it.

Success in the Characters

It was the relationship between the two men that offered a counter balance to the murder, detecting and trouble on the streets. Malden played Lt. Mike Stone, the older seasoned detective who grew up in San Francisco and knew the city and its people like the back of his hand. His partner, played by Douglas, was Steve Keller, a 28-year-old college graduate who was new to the police force. It was Stone's job to show Keller the ropes. After 20 years on the force, Stone wasn't really interested in breaking in a new detective, but he found a fresh set of eyes, a youthful attitude and a different approach were not to be overlooked. He referred to him as "Buddy Boy" most of the time but the two quickly grew on each other and found they both had something to bring to the table and

Malden was the seasoned star of the show, but the youthful Douglas held his own as the show found its audience.

could learn from one another. And soon they were friends off the job as well as on.

Stone was a widow who's college-age daughter Jeannie, played by Darleen Carr, made a number of appearances offering Mike Stone a life off the force, while Keller was known as a ladies man and his good looks and charm had him the object of many affections and gave the two men very different lifestyles off the job, but created a camaraderie and banter that provided relief against the seriousness of the storyline each week.

Filmed in the City by the Bay

The show was filmed almost entirely on location in the city and it celebrated the all aspects of San Francisco. From the Golden Gate Bridge to the popular waterfront and Union Square the show crisscrossed cable cars with hilly car chases and chase scenes at the airport and murders in Golden Gate Park or Twin Peaks.

Like its competitors, the show was not without a long roster of celebrity guests. Names like Dick Van Patten, Mark Hamill, Stefanie Powers, Martin Sheen, Tom Bosley, Tom Selleck, Larry Hagman, Bill Bixby, Norman Fell, Anthony Geary, Michael Constantine, Leslie Nielsen, James Woods, Nick Nolte, Arnold Schwarzenegger, Pat Conway, Patty Duke, John Ritter and Robert Wagner took to the streets at one time or another.

The series gave Michael Douglas the training ground to craft

The chemistry between the two actors helped the show succeed.

his talents as an actor and after four seasons on the series, he left the show for greener pastures. Departing after the second episode of the fifth season, Douglas had produced *One Flew Over the Cuckoo's Nest*, an Academy Award winning Best Picture in 1975 and he would go onto win another Oscar, this time as Best Actor for *Wall Street* in 1988. Both Malden and Douglas were nominated twice for Emmy Awards for their work on *The Streets of San Francisco*, as well as one nomination each for Golden Globes.

After Douglas' exit the show explained his absence by having him leave the force for a teaching position. He was replaced by an equally young and similar-looking actor, Richard Hatch, who took up where Douglas left off for the remainder of what would be the final season of the show. Fans reportedly didn't welcome the change and after 119 episodes and falling ratings the series ended on June 9, 1977.

NBC revisited the series in 1992 when they aired *Back to the Streets of San Francisco*. Karl Malden made a comeback for the show, but Douglas remained absent. The plot centered on Mike Stone investigating the murder of his longtime partner. Even though Steve Keller (aka Douglas) was missing, his presence is felt throughout the show. Since then DVD releases of several seasons and syndication of the show have continued to provide fans a chance to revisit San Francisco's streets regularly.

MURDER on the Boob Tube

MURDER on the Boob Tube

MURDER on the Boob Tube

MURDER on the Boob Tube

The Also Rans

They went that-a-way

Nearly since the advent of television the detective was on the case. While TV started as a live medium, once they began to record programming on videotape shows of all shapes and sizes were tested and aired. While budgets were often small, special effects limited and large sets uncommon, the detective was a viable choice. It only took a few actors, a small office and some darkened alleys and streetlights to provide the necessary atmosphere for hardboiled scripts that were relatively easy to film and produce. And as one concept caught on, a host of merry followers trailed behind copying a successful format and capture a lucrative audience that was looking for something to watch on this new electronic box in their living rooms.

Often one concept for a show would lead to a handful of similar series. If one public defender could find viewers as he got his clients off a case of murder, three more would follow as writers tried to capture the success. But for every *Perry Mason* or *The Untouchables* were a dozen failed attempts. Often the key to success was the timeslot, the writing, the lead in show, and of course the star.

And many successful actors, from Raymond Burr, John Cassavetes, Darren McGavin and David Jannsen would become stars with TV roles in the early days of television, while former film stars like Boris Karloff and Robert Taylor would find TV a place to transition to in their later years as film roles grew scarce. Here we offer a collection of some of the shows with murder a regular occurrence in the plot.

Many Ways to Tell a Tale

Martin Kane, Private Eye

Back in 1949 one of the first crime series, *Martin Kane, Private Eye* took to the airwaves. It showed an incorruptible, dedicated man who wouldn't stop until the crime was solved and the truth revealed. While the show lasted five seasons, it changed dramatically at it progressed. Four different actors played Martin Kane. First Lee Tracy, followed by Lloyd Nolan, William Gargan and Mark Stevens. Even the name of the show changed. After several seasons under the original name, the show was rechristened *The New Adventures of Martin Kane* and finally, for its final season, the show was simply called *Martin Kane*.

Man Against Crime

Also beginning in 1949 and fated to a six-season run, *Man Against Crime* starred Ralph Bellamy as Mike Barrett, a gun-toting detective out for truth and justice. Sponsored by R.J. Reynolds Tobacco Company, Barrett was often seen smoking throughout the show and in the early scenes star Ralph Bellamy would appear onscreen during sponsor breaks talking about veteran's hospitals that the sponsor was donating cigarettes to each week. But after five seasons, Bellamy exited the show and it seemed like *Man Against Crime* was through, but the series returned for one last season in 1956 when Frank Lovejoy took over the lead role.

Rocky King

In 1950 Roscoe Karns starred as police detective *Rocky King* in a show named after the title character. Also called *Inside Detective*, the show only aired periodically, producing about 9 shows between 1950 and 1954. It aired on the DuMont Television Network and in fact used the offices and hallways at the studio as sets for filming. He was a guy who had to rely on his brains rather than brawn to trap the bad guys and was known for having telephone conversations each episode with his unseen wife Mabel.

The Plainclothesman

Attempting to be novel, *The Plainclothesman* featured a Lieutenant played by Ken Lynch who never actually appeared camera, as the crime shows each week were told first person from his perspective and the camera acted as his eyes. It was a technique used in the 1947 film *Lady in the Lake*. The series aired in 1950 but the show never took off.

Mr. District Attorney

In 1951 *Mr. District Attorney* starred Jay Jostyn in the title role, which made sense since he had actually played the character in a radio version first. The show only lasted a season though and disappeared. But the series returned in 1954 and took another shot at success with David

Brian in the lead role, but the series only lasted about 8 episodes.

Mark Saber

Mark Saber aired under a few names during its run that began in 1951. Initially called *Mystery Theatre*, perhaps the success of title character shows like *Perry Mason* and *Martin Kayne* lead the producers to re-title show as *Saber* and *Mark Saber*. Played by Tom Conway, *Mark Saber* aired between 1951 and June 1959. He was an Englishman inspector helping out a U.S. metropolitan police department. He was assisted by a dedicated Sergeant Maloney and after the initial series ended the show was reformatted with Saber back in London helping Scotland Yard solve crime. The show seemed to air in syndication under a host of different names like *The Vise, Detective's Diary, Saber of London, The Vise: Mark Saber,* and *Uncovered*. When the show returned to the air in December 1955, it had a whole new cast. On this version, various Scotland Yard types would assist in solving difficult crimes, with Inspector Parker appearing frequently.

Doorway to Danger

Doorway to Danger debuted in 1953 with Stacy Harris as "an agent who investigates crucial social and political situations" according to its promotion.

Jimmy Hughes, Rookie Cop

Jimmy Hughes, Rookie Cop starred Billy Redfield as the title character in this DuMont Television network series. The series aired briefly in 1953.

The Man Behind the Badge

Similar to the *Plainclothesman*, *The Man Behind the Badge* featured narration of the nasty goings-on. This time Charles Bickford starred as the host and narrator of the crime drama. It aired first in October 1953 and lasted two seasons until, after 89 episodes, it ended in September 1955.

The Lineup

In October 1954, The Lineup began airing on CBS. Similar to Dragnet, the series took real stories from the San Francisco Police Department to offer a realistic documentary-like series of police officers in the city by the bay. Airing first for a half-hour and then expanded to one-hour in 1959 the series lasted until January 1960.

Wanted

In 1955 Walter McGraw starred in *Wanted,* a series that followed the F.B.I. on the hunt of some of their most wanted men.

Public Defender

Also in 1955 *Public Defender* starred Reed Hadley as a public defender who provided much needed legal assistance to people who couldn't afford a lawyer on their own.

Naked City

There were eight million stories in the *Naked City*, and the first one started as a feature film, but soon the show was turned into a series for television starring James Franciscus as a young handsome detective with John McIntire as the seasoned older cop. The show debuted in 1958 but in 1960 the cast was changed when Paul Burke took over the lead role supported by Nancy Malone and Horace McMahon. The retooling of the show lasted four seasons until spring 1963 and was highlighted by realistic New York street shooting of local landmarks and neighborhoods.

Colonel March of Scotland Yard

In 1958 Boris Karloff stepped off the big screen and into television as Colonel March of Scotland Yard. While Karloff had aged and the movie roles were few and far between, like many feature film actors the lure of a steady paycheck and a chance to continue performing had him moving to TV. In the series he starred as a British detective who used good science to solve the crime. Airing in 1956 the series only lasted one season.

Official Detective

Everett Sloane starred as a detective working on criminal cases that came from real police files in 1958.

Manhunt

Victor Jory as the private detective and Patrick McVey as his sidekick police news reporter teamed up for *Manhunt* which aired in 1959.

The Asphalt Jungle

John Huston's 1950 feature film *The Asphalt Jungle* carried the same title, but little else from the film made it into the television series starring Jack Warden. The show debuted in 1961. The series lasted only one season, producing 13 episodes.

Coronado 9

Coronado 9 was a syndicated series with Rod Cameron in the detective role that lasted for 39 episodes in 1960. Cameron actually had a few series where he played a similar role. *City Detective* aired for two seasons between 1953 and 1955 and *State Trooper* which aired between 1956 and 1959.

MURDER on the Boob Tube

The Lawless Years

In 1959 *The Lawless Years* debuted with James Gregory in the lead role as a detective in the 1920s battling against the underworld. The show lasted three seasons, ending in the fall of 1961.

Johnny Staccato

John Cassavetes starred as *Johnny Staccato* in this 1959 series. First airing in September, the series lasted for about 27 episodes until March 1960 with Cassavetes as a private detective. But when the show was first being developed he was reportedly supposed to be a jazz piano player.

The Detectives

Movie actor Robert Taylor came to television in 1959 in *The Detectives*. His partner in solving crime would go onto bigger fame in the latter part of the 1960s as the legendary cape-crusading superhero *Batman* – he was Adam West.

Decoy

New York City policewoman Casey Jones, played by Beverly

Darren McGavin starred as a crimescene photographer in one 50s series.

Garland, was often assigned to fight crime by going undercover in some of the seediest and most dangerous parts of New York. The syndicated series first aired in October 1957 and ran until early 1959 and was later aired under the name *Policewoman Decoy*. It was one of the first female-driven cop shows on television.

Peter Gunn

Craig Stevens starred in the title role of *Peter Gunn*, a series created by Blake Edwards that lasted for three seasons from 1959 until 1961. The series was popular enough to return in 1989 as a TV movie starring Peter Strauss.

Richard Diamond, Private Detective

Richard Diamond, Private Detective starred David Janssen as an investigator for four seasons from 1957 to 1960. Janssen would go onto later fame as a wanted man being sought for the murder of his wife in *The Fugitive*.

Crime Photographer

Darren McGavin who would go onto fame later in *The Night Stalker*, starred in *Crime Photographer* who worked for *The Morning Express*. The series aired in 1951 and was directed by Sidney Lumet.

Markham

Markham starred Ray Milland as a successful and wealthy lawyer who also found himself taking on the role of investigator to help free

The cast of 'The Untouchables. The series ran from 1959 to 1963.

his clients. The series aired 59 episodes from May 1959 and September 1960.

Sherlock Holmes

Also referred to as *The Adventures of Sherlock Holmes*, *Sherlock Holmes* first aired in 1954 with Ronald Howard as the famous detective and Howard Marion-Crawford as his dedicated side-kick Dr. Watson. The show aired from October 1954 to October 1955 with 39 episodes being produced.

Charlie Chan

Charlie Chan or *The New Adventures of Charlie Chan* debuted in 1957 with J. Carrol Naish starring as a Chinese-American detective called in to solve difficult cases. He was assisted by his son and the series first aired in August 1957 and after the first season began the show's production moved from the U.S. to the United Kingdom where it remained until the series came to a close in the summer of 1958.

The Untouchables

The Untouchables ran from October 1959 to May 1963 for four seasons with Robert Stack starring as Special Agent Eliot Ness who along with an team of dedicated agents battled organized crime in the 1930s in Chicago. The show's success was based in part on the realism of the portrayals and the grittiness of the stark black and white episodes. In 1960 the series earned an Emmy Award for Outstanding Achievement

'The Mod Squad' aimed at the young hip crowd in trying to win audiences over in the late 1960s.

in Film Editing for Television and its star Robert Stack a nomination for his acting. Stack would be nominated again in 1961 and the show would also be nominated again for film editing, but wouldn't win. And also in 1961 Elizabeth Montgomery would earn an Emmy nomination as supporting actress for her work in an episode. The series also earned a nomination for a Grammy Award for its music in 1961 as well as several Directors Guild nominations in 1960 and 1961. The series would become a longtime favorite in syndication as well and would return in 1987 as a feature film starring Kevin Constner and Sean Connery, as well as a TV series that lasted two seasons in 1993 and 1994.

Mike Hammer

Mike Hammer, also known as *Micky Spillane's Mike Hammer* was based on the writer's successful detective novels and lasted two seasons in the latter 1950s. The series starred Darren McGavin.

The Mod Squad

Debuting in September 1968 *The Mod Squad* took three outsiders and turned them into unusual agents for the police as they fought crime and solved murders as undercover agents. The show appealed to younger audiences with its attractive and youthful cast and lasted for five seasons from 1968 to 1973. They didn't always end up embroiled in murder cases but death was always close at hand. The show would earn six Emmy nominations including several for actress Peggy Liption as well as five Golden Globe nominations and Lipton would earn a Golden Globe for her work in 1971.

Kojak

Telly Savales starred in *Kojak* for five seasons beginning in 1973. As a hard-headed and bald, lolly-pop sucking tough guy, Kojak earned Savales an Emmy Award in 1975 and a Golden Globe Award in

1976 for his portrayal. The show would earn a host of Emmy and Golden Globe nominations, as well as other award nominations during its run. And in 2005 it would be revisited as an all new TV movie and series with Ving Rhames in the title role.

Police Woman

Angie Dickinson was lured to television in 1974 for *Police Woman*. Airing for four seasons, starting in September 1974 and ending in March 1978, Dickinson starred as one of the few women on the force tough enough for the rough stuff. The actress would earn Emmy nominations in 1975, 76 and 77 and the show would earn a total of 7 Emmy nods over its run as well as four Golden Globe nominations. Dickinson's only win was a Golden Globe in 1975 as Best TV Actress. The Show

The stars of 'Adam 12' on the cover of TV Guide.

co-starred Earl Holliman. The series got its start as an episode in *Police Story*.

The Rockford Files

James Garner was well known to audiences from his *Maverick* series a decade earlier, but in 1974 Stephen J. Cannell helped create a new persona for him named Jim Rockford. For six seasons, from March 1974 to January 1980 *The Rockford Files* followed the life of a detective struggling to make ends meet and solve crimes all while living in a trailer at the beach in Southern California. The show's success was purely due to Garner's witty and strong portrayal of Rockford. He was far from perfect, but managed to solve his cases. The series was nominated for a host of Emmys and Golden Globe and Garner earned an Emmy as Best Actor in 1977.

And Still More

Many other shows during the 50s, 60s and 70s would feature murder and death as a central plot line. Some of those include:

The 50s

Foreign Intrigue, 1951
Mr. and Mrs. North, 1952
Police Story, 1952
Racket Squad, 1952
I'm the Law, 1953
The Lineup, 1954
The Telltale Clue, 1954
The Lone Wolf, 1954
Paris Precinct, 1955

I Spy, 1955
Highway Patrol, 1956
Meet McGraw, 1957
M Squad, 1957
The D.A.'s Man, 1958
Lock Up, 1959
Brenner, 1959
Hawaiian Eye, 1959

The 60s

Surfside 6, 1960
Checkmate, 1960
The Brothers Brannagan, 1960
The Third Man, 1960
Tightrope, 1960
Target: The Corrupters, 1961
87th Precinct, 1961
The New Breed, 1961
Arrest and Trial, 1963
The Fugitive, 1963
I Spy, 1964
The Man from U.N.C.L.E., 1964
Honey West, 1965
Secret Agent, 1965
The F.B.I., 1965
Dak Shadows, 1966
Felony Squad, 1966
Adam-12, 1968

The 70s

MURDER on the Boob Tube

The Rookies, 1972
Banacek, 1972
Banyon, 1972
Toma, 1973
Police Story, 1973
Barretta, 1975
Starsky and Hutch, 1975
S.W.A.T., 1975
Dog and Cat, 1977
Vega$, 1978
Simon and Simon, 1978
Mrs. Columbo, 1979

MURDER on the Boob Tube

MURDER on the Boob Tube

MURDER on the Boob Tube

The New Breed

... And the beat goes on

The TV detective and our approach to murder on the small screen has certainly changed in the last 50 or so years. In the early days we saw a lot of loners, men dedicated to the task of uncovering crime and bringing murderers to justice. Over the next several decades they came in a variety of shapes and sizes. Through much of the 50s they were carbon copies of one another. Yes, the actors changed and a there were some who were detectives, or others who practiced law - and even a woman or two. And still others came at it through the role of a newspaperman or a photographer, but the general structure and concept didn't travel far and the shows were often quite similar.

As the 1960s took shape things were changing. First color was becoming much more common and it added a level of brilliance to the undertakings. Even with the bloody dead corpse, many of the shows had vibrant of color that brought them to life. In addition, the budget got better and the medium began to show its viability as a product that could earn money and acclaim. And as camera and sound equipment improved as did other technical aspects of production the shows moved off into more action-packed sequences and a host of locations.

But most of all perhaps, by the end of the 60s we had character driven shows with strong central detectives. We also has more visibility of women, minorities, disabilities and other differences that made shows different. The 70s capitalized on this as did the 80s. And as the decades wore on all these elements continued to evolve. While the central plot was still murder, the variety of murders and those who solved them changed dramatically. But even so, as we look at some of those that succeeded and some that did not we can see that strong characters, good production values and interesting viewpoints were the way to gain and audience's loyalty.

More Memorable TV Characters

Some of the more memorable shows of the new breed are chronicled here.

Murder She Wrote

Murder She Wrote starred Angela Lansbury as mystery writer and amateur detective Jessica Fletcher for twelve seasons from 1984 to 1996 on CBS network. It was followed by four TV films. The series would become TV's longest-running mystery series, and came from

Richard Levinson and William Link who tried a similar concept in the 70s with an author playing sleuth on the TV series *Ellery Queen*. While the series only lasted one single season, Levinson and Link thought the idea of a bestselling mystery novelist who solved murders had the potential to succeed. The character wasn't that far off from Agatha Christie or her Miss Marple character, and the series was a fairly traditional format like many of the shows that came before it. It was the performance of Angela Lansbury and the collection of guest stars that made the show work.

The show was originally conceived for Jean Stapleton of *All*

Angela Lansbury was a hit with her long-running murder mystery series 'Murder She Wrote' on CBS.

in the Family, but she decided she didn't want to do another television series. Doris Day was reportedly offered the part but turned it down and the offer then went to Lansbury. Guest stars on the series included William Windom, Tom Bosley, Jerry Orbach, George Clooney, Courteney Cox, Neil Patrick Harris, Kate Mulgrew, Leslie Nielsen, Joaquin Phoenix, Janet Leigh, Vera Miles, Tom Selleck many others. The success of the series would lead to a host of similar shows featuring older stars as would-be detectives including Andy Griffith in *Matlock*, Buddy Ebsen in *Matt Houston*, William Conrad in *Jake and the Fatman* and more.

Magnum P.I.

There was only *Hawaii Five-O* as a modern day Hawaiian detective series until Tom Selleck took on the role of Thomas Magnum in *Magnum, P.I*, A private investigator living in Oahu, Hawaii, the series ran from 1980 to 1988 on CBS picking up almost as soon as the former detective series left the air. It was a highly rated show that quickly earned a loyal following and got promotion and tie-in from CBS' other high-ranked detective series, *Murder She Wrote*. Nielsen Ratings found *Magnum, P.I.* in the top 20 U.S. television programs during its first five years.

In large part the success of the series was due to the charisma and good looks of its star Tom Selleck. The show made Selleck a heartthrob and a superstar in the 1980s. He won an Emmy Award in 1984 and a Golden Globe in 1985 for his portrayal of the detective.

Diagnosis Murder

Dick Van Dyke was well known to TV and film audience for decades but set his sights on murder when he took up residence as a doctor who seemed more involved in solving murders than saving lives. The series was a spin-off from another detective show, *Jake and the Fatman* and first aired in October 1993. It ran for 8 seasons producing approximately 178 episodes. Van Dyke's Dr. Mark Sloan was very much like the male version of Angela Lansbury's Jessica Fletcher in *Murder She Wrote* and the show both had similar plots and guest stars. The star's son Barry Van Dyke also took part in the series as a detective helping Dr. Sloan capture the bad guys. The series ended in May 2001. Three TV movies aired before the series was launched with two in 1992 and another in 1993 and two follow-up telefilms aired on CBS in 2002.

Law & Order

Looking at murder from both sides, *Law & Order* was a show with duality, as the first half centered most often on a murder and the detectives who solve the case while the second half of the show covered the case through the court system and legal proceedings that followed. Created by Dick Wolf, the NBC series debuted on September 13, 1990 and has since become the longest running drama on television. Set in New York City the show has earned critical acclaim and some 40 awards along with 149 nominations for everything from directing, casting, acting, writing and more. The series follows the professional careers and personal lives of police and prosecutors fighting crime in the beloved city.

Dick Van Dyke was welcomed back to TV for his series 'Diagnosis Murder' in the 1990s.

The success of the series resulted in a franchise of shows with several also becoming long-running primetime hits. *Law and Order* spin offs include *Law & Order: Special Victims Unit; Law & Order: Trial by Jury; Law & Order: Criminal Intent*; and *Conviction*.

CSI

CSI: Crime Scene Investigation premiered on CBS on October 6, 2000 and has since become another long-running series covering murders and those who solve them. It also launched a successful series of spin-offs becoming a big financial franchise for the network. The show was created by Anthony E. Zuiker and produced by Jerry Bruckheimer and takes place in Las Vegas. Other shows follow a similar format taking place in New York and Miami and follow the lives and work of groups of crime scene investigators and the techniques and skills they use to solve crime. It launched a new brand of show focused on the forensic side of crime. Unlike *Quincy M.E.*, the *CSI* shows are ensemble casts that are highly stylized and focus less on performance and the crime and more on the efforts to piece together the events surrounding the crime.

Nash Bridges

Don Johnson had roles in a few films and TV projects, but became a star when his NBC series *Miami Vice* hit television in the 1980s. After the end of the series Johnson moved to CBS for a detective series called *Nash Bridges*. Set in San Francisco, the show follows Johnson's detective Nash on the trail of bad buys and solving murders and sometimes other crimes. The series ran for six seasons from March 1996 until May 2001.

Cold Case

CBS was on a roll and anxious to keep the murder audience tuned in so a handful of other shows, including *Criminal Minds, Without a Trace* and others appeared alongside their *CSI* franchise to pad out the weekly prime time lineup so every day viewers had another mystery to solve. *Cold Case* followed a similar ensemble cast of detectives solving murders, but in this case they were unsolved crimes that happened years or decades earlier. Debuting in 2003, the show was still running some seven seasons later.

Women's Murder Club

Angie Harmon found success on *Law & Order* several years earlier and returned to the murder circuit as the star of *Women's Murder Club* on ABC in 2007. The series followed a band of women who formed a strong friendship and were bound together by the work they do – a detective, a lawyer, a coroner and a newspaper reporter. The series only lasted one season.

A Cast of Others

Many other shows have focused on murder in recent years with a focus on death in the plot line. Some series lasted longer than others. Shows like *Hill Street Blues, Cagney & Lacey, NYPD Blue, Murder One, Miami Vice, Silk Stalkings* and more. And many shows are still bringing in viewers including *Without a Trace, N.C.I.S., Monk, Burn Notice, Numbers, Castle, Bones, The Mentalist, Criminal Minds* and others.

MURDER on the Boob Tube

MURDER on the Boob Tube

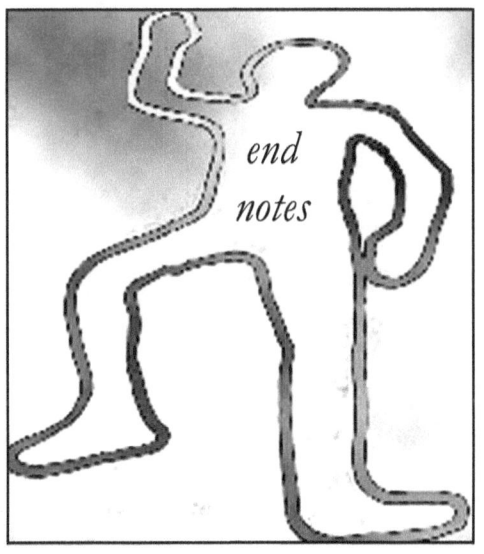

MURDER on the Boob Tube

Closing Remarks

Revisiting a classic but deadly past

Within the corners of our mind exists a place where all sorts of unexpected memories survive. While we expect to retain recollections of important moments in our lives, relevant dates in history and a host of things we've studied or actions we use daily, we also find vast memories of things we might never have expected we'd recall. Those song lyrics from music of our youth that seem to flow from us when we hear a favorite tune we haven't heard in decades or the movie dialogue, TV themes songs and even commercials that struck a cord and found a place in us where they would exist forever.

Something like that happens with our favorite TV shows as well.

While some classic shows have rightly earned a special place in our hearts, some shows, upon later viewing might not hold up to the memories we have of them. Perhaps in our youth we accepted it much more readily. Perhaps it was the time and place and the passage of time and the later shows and realities we see have somehow altered our perception. But even in those cases we often still carry a happy and hopeful memory of something that once meant more to us.

Murder on a Weekly Basis

And while it may seem strange for us to hold a fond or hopeful memory of a TV series that brought death and crime into our homes on a regular basis, many of these shows brought much more. From life lessons about repercussions from our actions to suspense, adventure, comedy and mystery, these shows may have helped up learn how to solve problems, overcome adversity or work with others to address challenging situations.

And if all that seems like a stretch at least we got to discover the beauty of *Charlie's Angels*, or enjoy the witty banter of Karl Malden and Michael Douglas on *The Streets of San Francisco*. We laughed at the silliness of *McMillan and Wife* and cheered at the justice served up by *Perry Mason* and *Ironside*. We also got to appreciate the talents of Peter Falk in *Columbo*, Buddy Ebsen in *Barnaby Jones* and Mike Conners in *Mannix* and enjoyed the paradise of Hawaii as well as the skill of Jack Lord in *Hawaii Five-O*.

With television now offering so many options, both new and old, we have a chance to see how much production values and levels have changed. We also see how much technology and society has changed, but because of all these changes we also have a chance to revisit many of these shows. Whether on late night cable networks or DVD releases, original versions of these classic TV shows give us a chance to reflect upon where we've come from and where we ended up. We can look to remember what we were like when we first saw these shows and how much we have changed. But we can return to the past with an innocence even if it is murder on our minds ... and on the boob tube.

William Conrad and Buddy Ebsen shared the screen crossing over each other's series for 'Cannon' and 'Barnaby Jones' in the 1970s. Both shows live on in DVD and syndication.

MURDER on the Boob Tube

MURDER on the Boob Tube

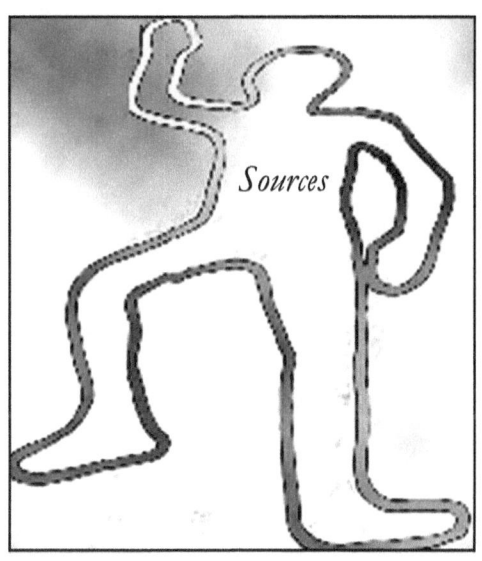

MURDER on the Boob Tube

Sources

Selected bibliography

A number of books, magazines, newspapers, documentaries and interviews, as well as the shows themselves provided sources of information and factual data that went into the writing of this book. Thank you to the many sources referenced throughout the book. There were many individuals whose work, insights, reviews, comments and suggestions that also helped make this book possible.

Books

Brooks, Tim and Marsh, Earle. *TV's Greatest Hits*. 1985. New York. Ballantine Books.

Campbell, Robert. *The Golden Years of Broadcasting*. 1976. New York. Rutledge Books.

Falk, Peter. *Just One More Thing*. 2006. DeCapo Press.

Finler, Joel W. *The Hollywood Story*. 1988. New York. Crown Publishers, Inc.

Harris, Warren G. *R.J. & Natalie*. 1988. Doubleday

Humphries, Patrick. *The Films of Alfred Hitchcock*. 1986. New Jersey. Crescent Books.

Kapsis, Robert E. *Hitchcock: The Making of a Reputation*. 1992. Chicago. The University of Chicago Press.

Moog, Ken. *The Alfred Hitchcock Story*. 1999. London. Titan Books.

Schwartz, Sherwood. *Inside Gilligan's Island*. 1988. St. Martin's Press.

Shulman, Arthur & Youman, Roger. *How Sweet It Was*. 1966. New York. Bonanza Books.

Spoto, Donald. *The Dark Side of Genius: The Life of Alfred Hitchcock*. 1983. New York. Ballantine Books.

Starr, Michael Seth. *Hiding in Plain Sight - The Secret Life of Raymond Burr.* 2008. Applause.

Weiner, Ed & Editors of TV Guide. *The TV Guide TV Book.* 1992. HarperCollins.

Magazines, Newspapers & Transcripts

Buckman, Adam. "The Oldest Living TV Star Just May Surprise You. November 19, 2006. The New York Post.

Clark, Neil. "So, You Want Democracy?" April 14, 2007. Morning Star

Deggens, Eric. "Where Have You Gone Barnaby Jones?" March 22, 2004. St. Petersburg Times.

Elber, Lynn. "New drama 'Leverage' lures Hutton back to TV." December 5, 2008. Lewiston Morning Tribune (Idaho)

Fillo, MaryEllen. "Odd Couple, Quincy Star Jack Klugman." October 12, 2008. Hartford Courant.

Maloney, Mike. "Tribute to Jack Lord." January 25, 1998. The People.

Natalie, Richard. "Buddy Ebsen." July 14, 2003. Variety.

Oei, Lily. "TV Land Raids Vaults on Viacom Siblings." April 25, 2002. Daily Variety.

Rodgers, Anne. "Gracious, Class 'RJ' Leaves E'm Sighing." February 26, 2009. Palm Beach Post.

Staff. "When Marriage was Just Plain Murder." November 1, 2008. Hudderdfield Daily Examiner.

Staff, "Jim Hutton, Actor, 45; Was TV 'Ellery Queen'." June 4, 1979. The New York Times.

Staff. "Q&A on the News." March 26, 2009. The Atlanta Journal-Constitution.

Verniere, Jim. "Ocean's Twelve is More Celebrity Travelogue Than Caper Film." December 10, 2004. The Boston Herald.

Internet Sources

Internet Movie Database, www.imdb.com

Wikipedia, www.wikipedia.com

New York Times, select.nytimes.com

Absolute Barnaby, liorshm.tripod.com/barnaby

Alfred Hitchcock Wiki, www.hitchcockwiki.com

CharliesAngels.com, www.charliesangels.com

The Ultimate Columbo Site, www.columbo-site.freeuk.com

TV Guide, www.tvguide.com

Photo Credits

The publishers wish to thank TV Guide for the use of selected covers from past issues featuring memorable detectives. In addtion, some photographs of TV shows and stars were acquired to complement the stories chronicled here. While some are part of the author's private collection it was difficult to determine rights or ownership for a number of the images used here. Any questions regarding the photographs can be directed to editors@aplombpublishing.com and photo credits can be provide for future updates of this publication. We gratefully thank all sources of the images that help tell the story.

MURDER on the Boob Tube

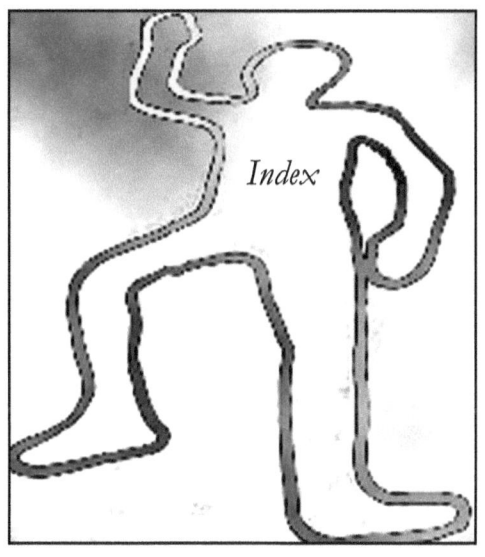

MURDER on the Boob Tube

Symbol

87th Precinct 197

A

Acker, Sharon 157
A&E Mystery Theatre 102
Arness, James 60
A-Team, The 82
ABC 67
Academy Award 181
Adam-12 92
Adventures of Ellery Queen, The 99
Adventures of Sherlock Holmes 193
After the Thin Man 107
Airport '79 110
Akins, Claude 45
Albert, Eddie 81
Alda, Robert 170
Alexander, Ben 91
Alfred Hitchcock Hour, The 34
Alfred Hitchcock Presents 29-36
Allen, Irwin 1, 241
Ameche, Don 101
Amos Burke, Secret Agent 53
Anderson, Barbara 127
Anderson, Richard 45, 157
Another Thin Man 107
Ansara, Michael 152
Arden, Eve 101
Arrest and Trial 197
Asphalt Jungle, The 190
Astin, John 152
Avengers, The 53
A Streetcar Named Desire 179
A View to a Kill 72

B

Badge 714 91
Ball, Lucille 136
Banacek 80, 197
Banyon 198
Barnaby Jones 39-46
Barney Miller 82
Barretta 198
Barry, Gene 51
Basigner, Kim 16
Bat Masterson 51
Baur, Elizabeth 127
Baxter, Anne 81
Baxter-Birney, Meredith 45
Begley Jr., Ed 170
Bellamy, Ralph 186
Belle Geddes, Barbara 33
Berle, Milton 101
Beverly Hillbillies, The 42
Bickford, Charles 188
Bisoglio, Val 165
Bixby, Bill 45
Bob Newhart Show, The 178
Bones 207
Born to Dance 41
Bosley, Tom 180
Breakfast at Tiffany's 42
Brenner 197
Brian, David 187
Bristol-Meyers 33
Broadway Melody of 1936 41
Broadway Televison, Theater 41
Brooks, Geraldine 45
Brothers Brannagan, The 197
Bullwinkle Show, The 60
Burke's Law 49-54
Burke, Paul 189
Burns, George 101
Burns, John 118
Burn Notice 207
Burr, Raymond 82

C

Cagney & Lacey 207
California Highway Patrol 88
Cameron, Rod 190
Campanella, Joseph 129

Cannell, Stephen J. 82
Cannon 57-63
Cannon, Glenn 115
Cannon, J.D. 141
Carr, Darleen 180
Carradine, David 129
Carter, John 39
Carter, Terry 141
Cassavetes, John 81
Cassidy, David 129
Cassidy, Jack 45
Castle 207
CBS 24
Chang, Christina 93
Charlie's Angels 16, 65-72
Charo 129
Chasing Farrah 72
Checkmate 197
Chevy Mystery Show, The 77
Christie, Agatha 203
City Detective 190
Clark, Dane 157
Clooney, George 204
Cobb, Lee J. 78
Colasanto, Nicholas 82
Cold Case 153
Coleman, Dabney 45
Collins, Ray 157
Colonel March of Scotland Yard 190
Columbo 15, 75-82
Connery, Sean 194
Conqueror, The 60
Conrad, William 43, 126
Constantine, Michael 180
Constner, Kevin 194
Conviction 206
Conway, Gary 49, 52
Conway, Pat 180
Conway, Tom 188
Coogan's Bluff 144
Coogan, Jackie 45
Cook, Carol 152
Coronado 9 190

Cotton, Joseph 33
Cox, Courteney 204
Crawford, Joan 136
Crimes Of The Hart 111
Crime Photographer 192
Criminal Minds 207
Cronyn, Hume 33
Crosby, Bing 15
Crosby, Cathy Lee 45
CSI 17
Culp, Robert 81

D

Dak Shadows 197
D.A.'s Man, The 197
Daniels, William 170
Dan August 61
Davis, Bette 136
Day, Doris 204
Days of Wine and Roses 167
Decoy 191
Dell Publishing 32
Denning, Richard 115
Desilu 136
Desperate Housewives 93
Detective's Diary 188
Detectives, The 191
Devlin Connection, The 154
Dhiegh, Khigh 115
Diagnosis Murder 53
Dickinson, Angie 195
Directors Guild 194
Disneyland 41
Dog and Cat 198
Doorway to Danger 188
Douglas, Kirk 179
Douglas, Michael 179
Doyle, David 69
Dragnet 87, 85-93
Dragnet 1967 91
Duggan, Andrew 118
Duke, Patty 180

DuMont Television Network 100
Dunaway, Faye 81
Duvall, Shelley 62
Dynasty 72

E

Eastwood, Clint 144
Eban, Al 115
Ebsen, Buddy 41
Ed Sullivan Show, The 33
Ellery Queen 97-102
Ellery Queen's Minute Mysteries 99
Ellery Queen: Don't Look Behind You 100
Ellis, Herb 91
Emergency! 92
Emmy Awards 33
Encore Mystery Channel, The 102
Endo, Harry 115
Ericson, John 53

F

Farrell, Sharron 115
F.B.I, 61
Falk, Peter 15
Fantasy Island 108
Farrell, Mike 62
Fawcett, Farrah 16
Fawcett-Majors, Farrah 70
Fear Strikes Out 179
Federal Communications Commission 26
Fell, Norman 180
Felony Squad 91, 197
Fisher, Gail 136
Flanders, Ed 118
Fong, Kam 118
Ford, Harrison 128
Ford Star Time 35
Ford Television Theatre 51
Foreign Intrigue 196
Forensic Detectives 170

Four Star Television 52
Fox, Michael 49
Francis, Anne 45, 53
Franciscus, James 189
Freeman, Leonard 118
Fugitive, The 192
Further Adventures of Ellery Queen, The 100

G

Galloway, Don 127
Gardner, Erle Stanley 159
Gargan, William 186
Garland, Beverly 191
Garner, James 196
Garrett, Eddie 165
Geary, Anthony 180
Geller, Bruce 136
General Electric Theater 167
George, Lynda Day 45
Geronimo 60
Giant 153
Gibney, Hal 90
Gifford, Kathie Lee 16
Gillette, Anita 165
Gilligan's Island 24
Gilliland, Richard 149
Gless, Sharon 128
Goff, Ivan 68
Goldberg, Leonard 68
Golden Globe 111
Goodbye Columbus 167
Gorshin, Frank 128
Grammy Award 194
Grant, Cary 16
Grant, Lee 79
Gregg, Virginia 33
Gregory, James 191
Grey, Joel 129
Griffith, Andy 204
Groom, Sam 170
Guardino, Harry 157

Gunsmoke 167
Gypsy 179

H

Hack, Shelly 69
Hackett, Buddy 170
Hadley, Reed 189
Hagman, Larry 45
Hale, Barbara 161
Hale Jr, Alan 129
Hamill, Mark 180
Hargrove, Dean 82
Harmon, Angie 207
Harrington, Al 115, 118
Harrington, Desmond 93
Harris, Neil Patrick 204
Harris, Stacy 188
Hart, Richard 100
Harts In High Season 112
Hart to Hart 16, 105-112
Hart To Hart Returns 111
Hatch, Richard 45
Hawaiian Eye 197
Hawaii Five-O 16, 42, 115-120
Hayes, Helen 118
Hayward, Susan 136
Held, Karl 157
He Walked by Night 88
Highway Patrol 196
Hillerman, John 97
Hill Street Blues 82, 207
Hingle, Pat 129
Hitchcock, Alfred 4, 9, 33
Holbrook, Hal 162
Holden, William 111
Holliman, Earl 195
Home Is Where The Hart Is 111
Honey West 53
Hopkins, Bo 129
Hopper, William 161
Horror at 37,000 Feet 42
Houseman, John 81

Howard, Ronald 193
Hudson, Rock 80
Huston, John 190
Hutton, Jim 100
Hutton, Timothy 102

I

I'm the Law 196
Ice Station Zebra 153
Inside Detective 187
Intertect 136
Ireland, John 170
Ironside 61, 123-129
Ito, Robert 169
It Takes a Thief 110
I Confess 179
I Could Go on Singing 167
I Dream of Jeannie 69
I Spy 196

J

Jackson, Kate 16, 69
Jake and the Fatman 62
James Bond 53
Jane Wyman Presents The Fireside Threatre 51
Jannsen, Richard 186
Janssen, David 62
Jimmy Hughes, Rookie Cop 188
Johnny Staccato 191
Johnson, Don 206
Jones, Carolyn 170
Jory, Victor 190
Jostyn, Jay 187
Jump, Gordon 152

K

Karloff, Boris 186
Karns, Roscoe 187
Katt, William 162
Keale, Moe 115
Keith, Brian 33

Kelly, Grace 126
Kennedy, George 129
Kennedy, John F. 23
Kibbee, Ronald 82
Kidder, Margot 45
Kirk, Phyllis 107
Klugman, Jack 17
Kojak 194
Kopell, Bernie 128
Kramer vs. Kramer 71

L

L.A. Dragnet 93
L.A. Law 82
Ladd, Cheryl 70
Lansbury, Angela 202
Las Vegas 72
Lau, Wesley 157
Lawford, Peter 100
Lawless Years, The 191
Law & Order 92
Law & Order: Criminal Intent 206
Law & Order: Special Victims Unit 206
Law & Order: Trial by Jury 206
Lee, Bruce 129
Leigh, Janet 81
Lemmon, Jack 168
Levinson, Richard 79
Lineup, The 196
Link, William 80
Liption, Peggy 194
Lloyd, Norman 33
Lockhart, June 170
Lock Up 197
Loggia, Robert 62
Lom, Herbert 118
Lombardo, Guy 101
Lone Wolf, The 196
Longoria, Eva 93
Lontoc, Leon 52
Lord, Jack 16
Lorre, Peter 33

Louise, Tina 62
Lovejoy, Frank 187
Love Boat, The 108
Loy, Myrna 107
Lucy 33
Lumet, Sidney 192
Lupino, Ida 45
Lupus, Peter 53
Lynch, Ken 187
Lyons, Gene 127

M

MacArthur, James 118
MacLeod, Gavin 118
Macnee, Patrick 53
Magnum P.I. 204
Maharis, George 45
Malden, Karl 178
Malone, Nancy 189
Man, The 119
Manhunt 190
Mankiewicz, Tom 109
Mannix 16, 133-138
Mantooth, Randolph 128
Man Against Crime 186
Man Behind the Badge, The 188
Man from U.N.C.L.E., The 197
Marconi, Guiglielmo 25
Marion-Crawford, Howard 193
Markham 192
Markham, Monte 118
Mark Saber 188
Marlowe, Hugh 100
Marnie 11
Marshall, E.G. 128
Martin, Ross 118
Martin Kane 186
Martin Kane, Private Eye 186
Mary Tyler Moore 178
MASH 91
Matlock 53, 204
Matthau, Walter 33, 168

Matt Houston 46
Maverick 42
McCloud 80, 141-146
McCord, Kent 92
McDowell, Roddy 45
McGavin, Darren 33
McGoohan, Patrick 81
McGraw, Walter 189
McMahon, Horace 189
McMillan 154
McMillan & Wife 80, 149-154
McVey, Patrick 190
Meet McGraw 196
Mentalist, The 207
Meriwether, Lee 43
Mettey, Lynette 165
Miami Vice 206
Micky Spillane's Mike Hammer 194
Miles, Vera 33
Milland, Ray 192
Miller, Lee 157
Mills, Donna 62, 152
Minow, Newton N. 23
Mission: Impossible 53
Mission Impossible 135
Miss America 43
Mitchell, Don 127
Mitchell, Thomas 78
Mod Squad 91
Monk 207
Montalban, Ricardo 118
Montgomery, Elizabeth 194
Morgan, Harry 91
Morton, Gary 136
Moses, William R. 162
Mr. and Mrs. North 196
Mr. District Attorney 187
Mrs. Columbo 82, 198
Muldaur, Diana 170
Mulgrew, Kate 82
Murder Investigation 93
Murder One 207
Murder She Wrote 16, 53

Mystery Movie 80
My Lucky Star 41
M Squad 197

N

Nader, George 100
Naish, J. Carrol 193
Naked City 189
Nash Bridges 206
NBC 25
NBC Mystery Movie 79
Nero Wolfe 62
New Adam-12, The 92
New Breed, The 197
New Dragnet, The 92
New Perry Mason, The 162
Nick At Nite's TV Land 102
Nielsen, Leslie 45
Night Gallery 42, 145
Night Stalker, The 192
Nimoy, Leonard 81
Nolan, John 165
Nolan, Lloyd 186
Nolfi, George 120
Nolte, Nick 45, 180
North, Sheree 62
Numbers 207
NYPD Blue 207

O

O'Loughlin, Gerald S. 170
O'Neill, Ed 92
O'Neill, Eileen 52
Odd Couple, The 168
Official Detective 190
Old Friends Never Die 111
One Flew Over the Cuckoo's Nest 181
On the Waterfront 179
Orbach, Jerry 204
Ordinary People 102
Oscar 181
Our Miss Brooks 51

Outer Limits, The 35

P

Palance, Jack 136
Paris Precinct 196
Parke, Evan Dexter 93
Parker, Maggi 115
Pearl 110
Peck, Gregory 16
Penny, Joe 62
Perry Mason 45, 157-162
Persoff, Nehemiah 118
Pfeiffer, Michelle 16
Philco Televison Playhouse, The 167
Phillips, Barney 91
Phoenix, Joaquin 204
Pillow Talk 153
Plainclothesman, The 187
Pleshette, Suzanne 109
Policewoman Decoy 192
Police Squad 62
Police Story 196
Police Woman 195
Pollyanna 179
Poor, Poor Ophelia 178
Powell, William 107
Powers, Stefanie 45
Pratt, Judson 62
Prescription Murder 78
Pringle, Joan 123
Psychiatrist, The 145
Public Defender 189

Q

Quincy, M.E. 17, 165-171
Quinn Martin Productions 61

R

Ragin, John S. 165
Reed, Robert 133

Reese, Tom 97
R.J. Reynolds Tobacco Company 187
Roman, Joseph 165
Racket Squad 196
Rains, Claud 33
Randall, Tony 168
Raye, Martha 152
RCA 25
Return of Ironside, The 128
Return of Sam McCloud, The 146
Rhames, Ving 195
Richard Diamond, Private Detective 192
Ritter, John 118
RKO 161
Roberts, Ben 68
Roberts, Pernell 128
Roberts, Tanya 71
Rockford Files, The 82
Rocky and His Friends 60
Rocky King 187
Rogers, Wayne 45
Rookies, The 69
Ross, Marion 129
Rush, Barbara 101
Ryan, Peggy 115

S

Scarecrow and Mrs. King 72
Seven, Johnny 123
Shear Genius 72
Sheena 72
Smith, William 115
Somers, Brett 157
Stratton, Albert 157
Strook, Gloria 149
S.W.A.T. 108
Saber of London 188
Saint James, Susan 80
San Francisco International Airport 145
San Francisco Police Department 127
Sarge 129
Sarnoff, David 25

Savales, Telly 194
Schlitz Playhouse of Stars 41
Schuck, John 128
Schwartz, Sherwood 24
Schwarzenegger, Arnold 180
Scotti, Vito 152
Seconds 153
Secrets Of The Hart 111
Secret Agent 197
Selleck, Tom 180
Shamley Productions 33
Shatner, William 33
Sheen, Martin 62
Sheldon, Sidney 108
Shera, Mark 44
Sherlock Holmes 193
Silk Stalkings 207
Simon and Simon 198
Six Million Dollar Man, The 69
Skerritt, Tom 62
Sloane, Everett 190
Smash-Up on Interstate Five 42
Smith, Jaclyn 16
Sorry Wrong Number 60
Soul, David 62
Spelling, Aaron 68
Spielberg, Steven 81
Stack, Robert 193
Stapleton, Jean 203
Starsky & Hutch 108
Starsky and Hutch 198
Stars over Hollywood 41
State Trooper 190
Stevens, Mark 186
Stewart, James 126
Strassman, Marcia 129
Strauss, Peter 62
Streep, Meryl 71
Streets of San Francisco, The 70, 175-181
Stroud, Don 92
Sudden Fear 136
Sullivan, Susan 129

Surfside 6 197
Suspicion 35
Sweater Productions 171
Swofford, Ken 97
Swtich 110

T

Talman, William 161
Target: The Corrupters 197
Taylor, Robert 186
Telltale Clue, The 196
That 70s Show 72
The Alley Cats 69
The Dick Powell Show 51
The New Adventures of Martin Kane 186
Thin Man, The 107
Third Man, The 197
This Man Dawson 60
Thomas Crown Affair, The 137
Tightrope 197
Till Death Us Do Hart 112
Time Magazine 67
TJ Hooker 108
Tobin, Dan 157
Toma 198
Toomey, Regis 52
Tracy, Lee 186
TV Land Award 138
Twilight Zone, The 35
Two-Minute Warning 168
Two Harts In 3/4 Time 112

U

Uncovered 188
Untouchables, The 193

V

Vallee, Rudy 101
Van Dyke, Barry 205
Van Dyke, Dick 81
Van Patten, Dick 180
Vegas 108

Vise, The 188
Vise: Mark Saber, The 188

W

Wagner, Lindsay 109
Wagner, Robert 16
Walberg, Garry 165
Walker, Nancy 153
Wall Street 181
Walter, Jessica 45
Wanted 189
Warden, Jack 190
Wayne, David 100
Weaver, Dennis 80
Webb, Jack 88
Wedemeyer, Herman 118
West, Adam 191
Weston, Carolyn 178
Where Has Love Gone 136
White, Morgan 115
Wickes, Mary 33
Windom, William 152
Wiseguy 82
Without a Trace 207
Wizard of Oz, The 41
Wolf, Dick 92
Wood, Natalie 110
Woods, James 180
Written on the Wind 153

Y

Yarborough, Barton 91

Z

Zuiker, Anthony E. 206
Zulu 118
Zworykin, Vladimir 25

About the Author

John William Law is a writer and journalist whose work has appeared in newspapers, magazines and books. He has worked on the staffs of daily, weekly and monthly publications. He is the author of numerous books and narrates a podcast on iTunes entitled *The Movie Files*. He has appeared on television and film documentaries discussing film history and on national public radio. He lives in San Francisco. His books and ebooks include:

Curse of the Silver Screen - Tragedy & Disaster Behind the Movies (1999, Aplomb Publishing)

Scare Tactic - The Life and Films of William Castle (2000, Writers Club Press)

Reel Horror - True Horrors Behind Hollywood's Scary Movies (2004, Aplomb Publishing)

Master of Disaster: Irwin Allen - The Disaster Years (2008, Aplomb Publishing)

Alfred Hitchcock: The Icon Years (2010, Aplomb Publishing)

Disaster on Film: A Behind the Scenes Look at Hollywood Disaster Movies (2010, Aplomb Publishing)

If you enjoyed this book, you might also enjoy *Alfred Hitchcock: The Icon Years*. Published by Aplomb Publishing, the book is available in print and ebook from our Web site at www.aplombpublishing.com or from major booksellers and online retailers like Amazon.com.

www.ingramcontent.com/pod-product-compliance
Lightning Source LLC
Chambersburg PA
CBHW031243290426
44109CB00012B/411